Thoughts and Observations: Improving Our Lives through Elevated Awareness

"BRAVO! Upon completion of reading an excerpt of *Land of the Free,* I give a standing ovation to the author, Afi Makalani. This article takes the American reader in a virtual conference room where all thoughts and beliefs about our freedoms are placed on the table and examined. Makalani, having the essence of a therapist, addresses each position on the freedoms of speech and self-expression: how Americans choose to protest and how Americans respond to them.

Makalani's reflections are logical, non-political, and backed with historical evidence. To the open mind, this well-written article is most enlightening to show the hypocrisy of supporting our first amendment rights, yet criticizing the use of them in response to a non-violent protest. This article clearly explains how patriotism is often measured with a double standard. I found it refreshing and most therapeutic during this time of social and political unrest."

Bridgette D. Williams, M.A.T.
Owner of Koa Publishing Company
Author of Honor Thy Spouse and Mama's Diary
Co-Author of Freeing My Soul by Amanda Boone-Brown
Co-Author of Racism Doesn't Matter by Dr. Steve Parson

Dedication

This book is written for those of us who want to improve our own lives as well as position ourselves to make the world a better place. Here is a collection of essays that will provide us with some tools to help make that happen.

© 2017, Afi Makalani

All rights reserved. This book or any portion thereof may not be reproduced or used in any manner whatsoever without the express written permission of the publisher except for the use of brief quotations in a book review.

Mind B. Free Publishing

Contents

1. Maurice White
2. How to Avoid Unnecessary Competition
3. Humility
4. What is "Black"
5. Black History Month
6. A Question of Age
7. "The Message"
8. Purple Reign
9. Prince and Rap Music
10. BET Scored a Home Run with Prince Tribute
11. Love, Family, Community and Purpose
12. Let Us Be Proactive
13. Love for Serena Williams
14. Responding to Hate
15. Uncle Larry's Views
16. Land of the Free?
17. What My Wife Has Taught Me
18. Four Things I Would Tell Young People
19. "The Truth"
20. "Introspection"
21. "Whirlwind"
22. Additional Thoughts
23. Quotes

Foreword

This book started as the result of a practice I formerly indulged in on Facebook. Each Wednesday, my day of leave from my job, I would post what I called my "thought for the day." Typically, it was something inspirational or my response to something that I considered to be a relevant event. At some point, I began concluding that maybe a far larger (and far more interested) group of people could be reached if I took these essays that I was writing and formed a collection of my thoughts. At that point I decided to write a book detailing my thoughts and observations. You will notice throughout the book that I speak on music, obtaining humility, the question of what constitutes "Blackness" and many other issues that I ponder upon from time to time.

My goal with this book is to stimulate thought. Additionally, I hope to prompt people to adjust their behavior, always with the thinking that we want to make the world a more humane place, one where our inherent divinity is a factor in all that we do. I think it is important for the sake of clarification to mention that when I use the term "European," that it is synonymous with "White." Likewise, when I use the term "African," I am speaking of a person that some would label "Black." Thirdly, when I use the word "Kemet," I am referring to the original name of the country that has been renamed "Egypt" by the Greeks (Kwesi, 1995).

I want to challenge us to dig deeper and to inspire us to recognize that we, the general population, have the power to make significant change take place on this planet. We must first, however, stop relying primarily on politicians to change our conditions. History has shown that far too often their promises are as empty as pockets with holes in them. We are the agents of change. We must identify what roles we each want to embrace to bring about that change and then go about the process of doing what we can.

Also, I do not make any claims to be anyone's counselor. I am not qualified to deal with emotional issues that impact one's daily interactions. I instead focus on surface level thoughts. Traumatic experiences that require a deeper level of inquiry into someone's personal experiences is beyond the scope of this book.

Lastly, I want to show my appreciation to several people whose belief in me has allowed me to bring this series of essays into existence. These people include Prince and Margaret Reid Sr., Mavis Reid, Karnessa and Maurice Stover, Kacie Reid, Alvin Hill, Morgan and E.J. Newman, Earl Reid, Brenda Leigh Reid, Shelli Cumber, Nathaniel and Bessie Davis, Yolanda Ellis, Tara Croom, James Buggs, Harrison Bodrick, Eddie Robinson, Diallo Moss, Kevin Sabio, James and Audrey Duck, Larry Sledge, Delvin "D.I.P" Edmonds (R.I.P) and Marvin Roane, Sr. A special shout out goes to Marvin Roane, Sr. who told me that I was "special" and put me in positions to grow and evolve while we were members of The National African American Empowerment Association (NAAEA). Also, much love to my cousin (Judy J. Walden) who proofread and edited this book.

I hope you all find this labor of love to be beneficial in some way.

Peace.

Maurice White

As of this current date, February 11, 2016, we have seen a seemingly recent increase in the passing (deaths) of many of our musical heroes. The names include Natalie Cole, Glenn Frey, David Bowie, Nicholas Caldwell and most recently, Maurice White, mastermind of the great funk/soul/r&b band we know as Earth, Wind and Fire (EWF). Mr. White's death had a deep impact on me. Apparently, his departure affected others similarly, if we are to determine by the extensive number of Facebook posts made concerning him. People often shared posts of some of the classic songs performed by Maurice White and EWF. Accompanied by the posts of album covers or classic singles were peoples' own admission of love for the group and sadness to have to acknowledge Mr. White's transition to the spirit realm. I, too, felt the need to post something to show my love and admiration for Maurice White, EWF and the music to which they gave birth. However, I concluded that a Facebook post by me would do no more than duplicate what everyone had already done. I wanted to do more, so I decided that one of my essays in these collections of thoughts would be dedicated to the divine spirit we came to know and love as Maurice White.

I decided that to simply leave a Facebook post in honor of Mr. White would be insufficient for me. He and EWF's spirit have affected me too deeply to confine my gratitude to a single online post. I decided to attempt to perpetuate what Maurice White and EWF taught us. I wanted to somehow figure out a way to embody the spirit of this wonderful musical collective in a practical and sustainable way. Here is what I have decided to do.

Being an artist myself, I have concluded from years of observation, and introspection, that an artist's songs (especially if the artist is lyrically transparent) serve as minor journals, records of what an artist thinks or feels at a particular moment in time. EWF's lyrics are particularly honest and revealing. Therefore, it stands to reason that since Mr. White wrote and produced many of EWF's songs, if we listen to several of the songs that he and his band brought into existence over the years, we may be able to develop a fairly solid understanding of what made Maurice White "tick." Fueled by this reasoning, I have decided to do this. I started digging through all the EWF music I had at my house and combined that with some online research. I then started compiling a list of some of the group's most memorable (in my opinion) songs over the years. These are some of the titles that I introduced to my list:

1. Keep Your Head to the Sky
2. Where Have All the Flowers Gone
3. Mighty Mighty
4. Devotion
5. Reasons
6. Kalimba Story
7. All about Love
8. Spirit
9. Love's Holiday
10. Be Ever Wonderful
11. Serpentine Fine
12. Fall in Love with Me
13. Can't Hide Love

This is just a small sample of EWF songs. They have created many more breathtaking performances than just the thirteen that I have listed. I simply wanted to gather a song sample large enough to help with my next step in trying to identify a practical way to pay homage.

The next thing I have done is sat quietly and listened to all the songs I have listed with the goal of identifying the ideas or themes guiding each song. In doing so, I have striven to identify the essence of Maurice White and EWF, since as I said before, songs often serve as miniature journals. What I have concluded is that Maurice White was all about love, spiritual awareness and knowledge of self and history (as evidenced by the Kemetic images on albums). Now that we have a solid understanding of the inner workings of Mr. White, we can endeavor to find ways to apply his characteristics.

For instance, we have concluded that Mr. White was driven by love. I do not believe his love was only about romance. I think his love would also consist of love for friends, family and community. So now we must ask ourselves how we can apply love. Well, I think being more loving in a romantic way is the simplest and most immediate application. I will not get too specific about making suggestions in your romantic behavior. I will leave that up to each individual's creativity. But I will say that we should make a conscious effort to open our hearts more. I believe love is one of the most potent forces in the universe. It can heal and transform. It can give us the strength to carry on through troubling circumstances. Let us embrace it and the power it provides. Let us also demonstrate a higher level of love for friends and family by attempting to find quality time to spend with them. When everyone else betrays you, you often find that family and true friends will not forsake you. Furthermore, our interactions with them reconnect us to something real and meaningful in a world driven my materialism and deception, thus possibly keeping us more rooted in a place of sanity. I also think we can be more loving by trying to work to improve our communities. Maybe we can be mentors to the youth, particularly those that are products of challenging socio-economic environments. Maybe we can donate a few hours each week helping children with their reading or homework. Let us consider creating safe houses, places where children in tough communities can study and learn and not feel threatened. We could make sure these safe houses have computer access for the children who may not be able to afford their own PCs. We could consider providing classes that teach basic PC skills to minimize this digital divide we occasionally hear about. Continuing with this idea of showing community love, we could join organizations that are actively doing things to help our respective cities. As Maurice White once famously said: "if there aint no beauty you gotta make some beauty, have mercy." This is love-consciously working to make things better.

Another character trait that I concluded that Maurice White possessed was the desire to pursue spiritual awareness. I do not think I need to say much about us doing the same. There is so much literature that exists that can elevate our spiritual selves. There are study groups and spiritual collectives that can assist with our spiritual journey. We simply must keep searching and I believe the answers will start to reveal themselves.

A third attribute that Maurice White seemed to radiate was knowledge of self and history. Knowledge of self is something that can be linked with spirituality. I believe that we are all derived from the same source. Therefore, we are essentially the same. This flesh that encases our souls gives us the illusion of separateness, I believe. So, in studying ourselves and what makes us respond in certain ways to certain interactions and stimuli, we in turn develop a better understanding of why others respond in a certain way to certain situations or stimuli. I think this type of awareness gives us a better understanding of one another and positions us to be more empathetic to others, and to me, empathy is a step closer to sympathy. So, in studying ourselves, it ultimately gives us a chance to become more humane on a planet where inhumanity is all too common. As far as knowledge of history goes, I think he meant African or Black history. This is not to de-emphasize the contributions of any other ethnic group. But the reality is that it has been the contributions of people of African descent that has been consciously suppressed. Logic dictates, therefore, that the history of African people is the aspect of history that deserves the most consideration.

Lastly, we must acknowledge that EWF is one of the great bands of the 20th century, combining jazz, funk, blues, gospel, soul, African rhythms and disco. They have demonstrated some of the finest lead vocals (Maurice White and Phillip Bailey) with pitch perfect backing harmony. They have displayed some of the best musicianship you can imagine. Their lyrics often have provocative messages that challenge the listener. Needless to say, EWF pushed the envelope. Their induction into The Rock and Roll Hall of Fame was inevitable. Now we as artists must grab the baton and continue the musical race that EWF initiated. We too must dig deeper. We must study our respective genre and know the history of it, much like EWF was aware of the musical giants that preceded them and used the contributions of their predecessors to serve as their starting point to which they would add their own innovations. If we do all these things, the pain of Maurice White's departure may be decreased by the awareness that we are personifying what Mr. White represented. Therefore, his essence will continue to live through us.

How to Avoid Unnecessary Competition

Peace, family. I must share this with you. I hope this information is beneficial to someone.

I have noticed on numerous occasions that many people in this society judge their self-worth or value against how they stand relative to someone else. This type of self-definition leads to unnecessary competition. Many times, these chronic competitors almost seem to live for the moment when they can say: "I am faster than you." "My car is bigger than yours." "My dude/chick is built better than yours." Some of these same people are so inclined to act this way that you do not have to say anything at all. You can simply show up in a new pair of trousers without uttering a word and someone will specify, unsolicited, that their pants cost more than yours, or maybe they got a better price than you. What's the solution?

Well, I tend to approach things from a spiritual perspective. I truly believe that we have come into being for a reason. I think most of us are trying to bring meaning and significance to our existence. Unfortunately, we aren't taught how to go about finding out "why I am here" (your purpose). I also think that most of us are trying to find a way in this life to say **"I AM"**- I exist, I am important, I am meaningful, I contribute, hear me. In the absence of a means to say, "I Am," we struggle to find ways to stand out that are not necessarily helpful or pleasant for others to experience. Again, what is the solution?

I suggest that those of us who have not found our calling should find a quiet space. Cut off the television, radio and computer. Inform your loved ones that you need 30 minutes to an hour of free time to work on some things.

Break out a pen and pad and jot down all your passions-things that electrify your soul, your hobbies or interests that you will indulge in for free simply because it feels good to you. Next create a column where you list all the things that you seem to do well naturally. When you notice that some of your passions coincide with things that you do well or have been told that you do well, highlight them. Many spiritual teachers suggest that it is at this point that you may have just identified your **LIFE PATH**. Other spiritual teachers would call it your **DESTINY** or your **PURPOSE**. This could very well be the reason that you have been manifested into flesh in this realm of existence.

This is such a critical moment-when you identify your destiny. What you have now done is positioned yourself to bring more joy into your life. So many of us never find our purpose or destiny, so we spend decades working at a job that provides no excitement, reward or challenge for us. By becoming mindful of your passion, along with your purpose, you can go about the process of trying to find a way to indulge in it, if only on a part time basis. As you become more active in living your destiny, the need to say "hear me" is being addressed by the work that you are doing in your life path area. Therefore, the need to impress upon others how good you are will likely diminish. You will now be more inclined to move through life with a silent confidence, strength and tranquility.

I want to suggest one more thing as it relates to competing with others. Consider trying to compete with **yourself** instead of others. You may ask how and why I should attempt to compete with myself instead of others. Well, we have already discussed the tendency of many of us with no means of saying **I Am** (and I have been guilty of this myself) to compete over things that have little importance. What is worse is that as I have stated earlier, we tend to think in relative terms. We tend to perceive of ourselves relative to someone else. The problem with this type of thinking is that much like any competition, for someone to win, someone must lose. For far too many, to feel good about themselves, someone else must struggle or fail at a particular thing. In fact, I have observed some people who seem to relish in other people falling short in certain instances, so much so that they smile upon being informed that others have not met a certain objective. I do not think it is a good idea to derive pleasure from others' misfortunes. The Karmic relationship that you establish with the Universe by indulging in such thinking will, in my opinion, do you more harm than good.

So, how does anyone compete with themselves and not others, you may ask? Here is my suggestion, based on my own efforts to be a more pleasant individual.

We have already discussed making a list of our passions. Okay, let's say you have a passion to be a better basketball player. Instead of being jealous of others who are performing at a higher level than yourself, why not write down as many characteristics of a basketball player that you can think of. Some of these attributes may include dribbling with both hands, free throw shooting, rebounding, passing, outside shooting, shooting off the dribble going left or right, mid-range shooting, post moves, ability to lay the ball of the glass with both hands, defense, stamina, foot speed, jumping ability, strength, size or body mass, etc. Look at each of the characteristics that you have listed. Grade yourself from 1-5 on each aspect listed, 1 being the lowest and 5 being the highest you can receive in any area. Keep it simple. Look at the basketball skill (s) for which you have given yourself the lowest grades. If there are many areas that need work, just choose the two that you think deserve the most immediate attention. If for instance your jumping ability and foot speed need improvement, seek out sources of information pertaining to improving your performance in those deficient areas. In fact, be specific. Have someone time your 40-yard dash and have someone measure your vertical jump. Once you have obtained this information, let these measurements serve as the baseline of performance from which you start. Once you are aware of the drills and exercises in which you will participate, began doing them consistently. Have yourself measured again every two weeks and compare your most recent performances with your original baseline numbers. Eventually you will see an improvement in both your speed and jumping ability. This will have a profound effect on your game. If there are other areas that need enhancement, just follow the same formula we just discussed. Soon, you will feel like an entirely new basketball player, and it will all be possible because you competed against yourself (baseline performance), while not subjecting anyone else to unneeded competition.

I truly think that if we do these things, we will see a change in our lives, our success level, and a change in the perception that others have of us. This could very well lead to change in how people treat us. And lastly, these types of adjustments just may lead to a change in terms of how we think of ourselves.

Humility

I have written this essay on **humility** to come directly behind the previous essay ("How to Avoid Unnecessary Competition") because I think that the subject matter of the two are related. But before I go further to attempt to connect them, let us look at a definition of the word "humility" as provided by *Webster's New World Dictionary*.

Webster's identifies humility as: "the state or quality of being humble." So if humility is the "**state** or **quality** of being humble," what does it mean to be humble? Webster's also provides that definition. The definition given for the state of being humble is: "having or showing a consciousness of one's shortcomings; modest." What does this mean from a behavioral standpoint? Well, one could interpret someone to be conducting themselves in a humble way if they are quiet and reserved in speech. This may be partly true, but there is another part of the definition that must be addressed. Certainly it can be beneficial at times to be quiet and reserved in speech, but the definition for the world "humble" also suggests that we are to be mindful of our "shortcomings." That simply means that we must be conscious of the fact that none of us (me included) knows everything or can do everything. Therefore, we should be willing to accept advice or assistance from well meaning (and well-studied) associates who have more experience in certain areas of life than ourselves. An inability to be receptive to this assistance clearly is opposed to the strict definition of the word "humble," and suggests that regardless of how quiet or reserved we may be in outward expression, our refusal to consider help when needed indicates that humility has not been truly demonstrated in that instance.

What is the cause of this? We spoke in the previous essay about the need of people to say "**I Am**" (I exist, I am important, I am meaningful, I contribute, hear me). I think that in many cases, people have not identified their means of saying "I Am." I think that this leads to many of us feeling invisible, so we do all that we can to be seen or heard. Sometimes this includes disregarding the input or assistance of others at all costs, as long as our contributions take priority. But in finding our destiny or life path, we simultaneously find a means of saying **"I Am."** In doing so, our need to make more "noise" to be heard and seen will likewise be diminished.

You may ask are there other means to obtain a state of humility. I think that there are other examples of people obtaining a state of humility that are worthy of discussion. Hopefully in doing so, we can be more empowered to move in the correct direction.

What I want to do is cite a certain example of an individual transforming to a state of humility and talking about what prompted that change. I also want to discuss other people who have shown humility upon first meeting them. The goal is to determine if there are commonalities amongst the two (similar life experiences, opportunities, successes, etc.). My thinking is that if there are commonalities among these individuals, then at the very least we can see that there is some correlation between those commonalities and the acquisition of humility. I am not saying that there is a direct correlation as proven by statistical study. But if there is some coincidence that becomes evident, I think it wise to ponder the meaning and impact of it.

I remember a female peer of mine who was heavy set growing up. Needless to say, she was not always the receiver of positive attention from her male peers. I noticed that she would often compete in every way possible with her female peers, whether it was in foot races, academic performance or simply getting noticed by young boys. However, something interesting occurred with the young lady. She lost weight. As she did, the boys who had once disregarded her began to notice her. More frequently she was greeted with "hellos" and smiles from the same young men who had previously seemed not to notice her. Subsequently, with people starting more and more to recognize her physical appeal, she grew less interested in competing over things. She also appeared to become quieter. Yes, she would speak and be pleasant. She just seemed to no longer have a desire to be as loud as she once was. She radiated a level of quiet confidence and poise that had been previously lacking. Here we notice one of the possible experiences that seem to precede humility: a departure from feelings of invisibility (something we touched on earlier).

Another personal experience of mine pertaining to humility concerns my interactions while attending the "Y" (YMCA) and other fitness facilities.

Being that I am a slim man, it is unlikely that I am ever going to bench press 400 pounds. I do not have the mass or physique for that. This is totally fine with me. However, one acquaintance of mine (let's call him Antoine) who attended the same fitness facility seemed to derive a great deal of joy from acknowledging that I did not have enough weight on the bar whenever I was working on the incline bench press. He laughed heartily each time he saw me on the equipment. He then would bring it to the attention of his buddies who were in the gym with him. I thought it was a strange response. This dude outweighed me by sixty pounds. Why should I be able to lift as much as he could? Besides, I was not concerned with being a power lifter or a body builder. I just wanted to stay lean, fit and hopefully develop some respectable level of muscle definition. An interesting fact that is worth noting is that this dude by no means had a perfect physique himself, so what made him think he was in a position to be insulting to anyone. As far as I knew, he was not a personal trainer, had not won any body building competitions or power lifting competitions. I thought it was odd that he felt comfortable operating from such a condescending perspective, especially considering that he had done nothing noteworthy as it pertains to physical development. Furthermore, I never found it necessary to compare the amount of weight I lifted to how much he worked with, so his verbal slights always came with no provocation. I was always left scratching my head trying to make sense of his behavior.

Years later, I would work out at a "Y" not far from my present home. As usual, you have many different people who attend, both regularly and infrequently. Some members are young. Some members are older. Some are current athletes. Some are people who have never been athletically inclined. Some are striving to obtain more muscle mass. Some want to lose weight. Some are former body builders, and some played college sports and were members of semi-professional teams. Obviously, there are large numbers of different types of people who attend the "Y' and possess different backgrounds, interests and motivations for working out. I enjoy the diversity. Much like the variety of different backgrounds and life experiences that people at the "Y" bring to the table; you find a wide range of communication styles that exist when interacting with the different members. Some of these members are great listeners, waiting patiently for you to say what is on your mind before they respond. Other members frequently cut off your speech before your sentence is completed. Some members are very well read and speak about a variety of thought provoking issues from politics to spirituality. Other members prefer to indulge in less revealing conversations.

Here is where it gets interesting. I find that some people greet you at the gym with warmth and friendliness. Needless to say, I enjoy meeting these people each time I go to the gym. Other members seem to have nothing but insults to provide. Much like Antoine at the workout facility that I attended years back that operated from a negative perspective, I have found one individual in particular at my current "Y" that has nothing to bring forth other than insults. If I am doing cardio, he must acknowledge that I am not working out hard enough, as evidenced by my lack of sweat. Well, as I said before, I am lean and cold natured. So I do not sweat much unless I am outside and it is extremely hot. Furthermore, I have played sports all my life and I continue to stay relatively fit, so my body is conditioned well enough so that only an excessively challenging workout will bring me fatigue and make my sweat pour.

Another nagging tendency of this individual is his response to my interactions with females. If one of the female attendees at the gym has an extensive conversation with me, he will not hesitate to inform me that the female could not possibly find me attractive as I am too old or lacking some other characteristic that might garner a female's attention. No, I am not seeking any type of relationship with any females at the "Y" as I am happily married. That's not the point. The concern I have is that this guy has a never ceasing desire to insult me, much like the gentleman we discussed earlier. Some may ask what this dude looks like. You might imagine him having the looks of a top model for him to be so insulting. In fact, the very opposite is true. This guy (I'll call him Bob) is all of 5'6 and probably exceeds 310 pounds. I would imagine that if he stands perfectly erect and looks down, he would be unable to see his own feet. Now I don't say this to be hurtful. I simply want to provide a visual of Bob who despite his own obvious imperfections can't seem to be more tactful with what comes out of his mouth, at least when it comes to me.

Now before I go further, I want to acknowledge that Bob and Antoine both love to indulge in belittling comments, and both seemed to have little going on in their lives other than the ordinary. Some may suggest that jealousy was the cause of Antoine's behavior and that jealousy is the source of Bob's statements. I prefer to stay humble and not perceive of myself as anyone that would prompt envy, but I must concede that jealousy often does inspire people to take verbal shots at others to try to knock them off the pedestal on which they have mentally projected others to reside. However, I also am aware that there are those who may lack ideal physical features (as defined by this society's standards of attractiveness), yet they radiate a certain comfort with themselves. Why is this?

What I want to do going forward is focus on some other people I have met. Some of them have been gym attendees that I have come to know over the years. These mutual attendees to the "Y" consist of a former power lifter. Another gym member received a scholarship to play college football. Other people I want to consider are individuals that I have worked with in community driven projects. Some are studio engineers/song producers who are directly responsible for creating some of the best hip hop instrumentals to ever spring from the state of Virginia. I have a good friend who has self-published several books. The funny thing is that each of these individuals is extremely humble. They may discuss their past accomplishments, but the expression of their experiences never comes from a condescending place. They instead speak from the perspective of simply informing you of their interests or past activities. Over the years I have pondered the level headed and humble communication styles of these individuals. I have made efforts to determine what it is that makes these people different in how they approached others. Logically it would seem that since they have done things that are worth noting, they would be more inclined to be boastful, arrogant or insulting to those that they perceived did not measure up to their personal resumes. I thought about this long and hard until I started making certain connections, started noticing certain common denominators in those that exude humility. I also began noticing certain similarities among others who have been more prone to lack humility. This is what I have discovered.

Those that compete excessively or lack humility tend to:

1. Lack the means of saying "I Am" (check the previous essay)
2. Suffer from a sense of real or perceived invisibility

3. Demonstrate a lower than ideal self esteem

People that show humility often:

1. Have developed a means of saying "I Am"
2. Have accomplished noteworthy objectives or are actively doing so
3. Appear comfortable in their own skin

What does it all mean? If nothing else, those of us attempting to be humbler in our personal expressions should observe the correlations between developing a means of saying "I Am" with obtaining a state of humility. We should also be mindful of the impact that achieving goals and doing things of note has on our ability to be humble. Lastly, let us be mindful that much of this appears to be interrelated, in that those that develop a means of saying "I Am" may in turn achieve things of note which subsequently elevates the self-esteem which minimizes the need to be heard or diminish others.

Are these conclusions reflective of an exact science? I would say no because human behavior is extremely complex. However, we do want to increase our awareness of tendencies and correlations that will give us an improved understanding of how we can try to maximize our human potential. In this case, the focus is the attempt to identify some factors that will help us express ourselves with more humility. I hope this essay along with the previous one gives us some additional tools in moving in that direction.

What Is "Black"

(I want to clarify that my usage of the term "Black" in this essay does not indicate that I think that this word is the ideal one to describe or label African descended people. Some people prefer the label "African." Some prefer "African-American." Some may prefer the usage of "Nubian" or "Moor." My goal as a communicator is to express myself with as much clarity as possible. This often means using language that is most commonly used and expressed by the general population. I do not want us to get so hung up on labels that we miss the intent of the essay.)

This is an interesting question, right? It is funny because I am not sure any other ethnic group other than people of African descent grapple as much with this concern. Honestly, I do not hear Asians asking, "What is Asian?" And while some people of European descent probably show some resentment to fellow Europeans for not acting as "White" as they would prefer, I am not sure the pain is as severe for the maverick European as it is for a person of African descent. When you consider all the things that have been done historically to divide African people and the subtler tactics practiced today to promote our lack of solidarity, I would assume that we can all agree that Black folks (people of African descent) are the least prepared to deal with a lack of unity. What I would like to do with this essay is speak to why it seems so important to so many African people to act "Black." I will also endeavor to discuss how we can go about the process of redefining what constitutes "Blackness" so that the new definition and the corresponding behaviors are in line with the uplift of our people.

Before we can go forward, I think we must often go to the past. We must establish a firm understanding of history and the events that have taken place that serve as the manufacturers of the current mental, spiritual, economic, political and cultural climates in which we reside. Let us remember that the enslavement of people of African descent came with great costs. African people were forced to separate themselves from their indigenous forms of spiritual worship. Our native names and languages were forcibly stripped from us. Families were torn apart, and members were sold to other parts of the country with no hope of ever seeing one another again. Our indigenous meals and styles of food preparation were denied us. Our culture and traditions were taken away, as we know that any African (slave or free) who was observed practicing non-European traditions was greeted with severe consequences. Nothing happens in a vacuum. Certainly, there must have been repercussions that resulted from this comprehensive attack on the existence of African people. Specifically, we want to talk about the impact that this slavery has had on our strong desire to label behavior as "Black" or something other.

I want to once again seek the assistance of *Webster's New World Dictionary*. I want to clarify how *Webster's* strictly defines the word "culture."

Webster's defines culture as: **the skills, arts, etc. of a given people in a given period; civilization.** I will add that this entails the **variety of ways of communication, dress, slang, dance, forms of greeting, spiritual practices, etc. that are acceptable by a certain group that is often bonded by common physical features, geography and**

similar socio-economic conditions. Prior to the colonization of African countries and the enslavement of transplanted Africans from the continent and prior to the enslavement of Africans who have resided in North America and South America for 52,000 and 56,000 years respectively (Imhotep, 2011), we had our own culture. Our specific means of communication, dance, forms of greeting and spiritual systems were practices that were created and perpetuated by us. These practices were not imposed on us by foreign people. In addition, these practices were seemingly created for the collective forward movement of our African people. Social Science tells us that when a people are stripped of a culture, the need to have a collective means of expression that makes sense within that group will naturally occur. This is what has happened, in my opinion, to Black Americans. We have had our native cultural expressions removed by Europeans, so we naturally started creating a sub culture. We had to develop a collective means of intermingling with one another that allowed us to continue to exist. We needed to find a way of saying this is "Black."

Some people have argued that we have no culture. I disagree. While I concede that much of our African culture has been lost, I think we must likewise concede that we have in fact created many different means of expression that are acceptable and makes sense within the confines of our specific ethnic group (the very definition of culture). For instance, yes, we lost much of our original musical expression, but in response we have created Blues music, Gospel, Soul, Funk, Rhythm and Blues, Reggae, Calypso, Rock and Roll, Doo Wop and Rap. Our memories of our native forms of dance have been removed so we created Tap, Breakdancing, Pop Locking, Chicago Stepping and too many different popular dances to name. We have more methods of greeting one another than any other ethnic group. The different types of greetings include hand slaps, high fives, head nods, finger points, fist bumps, and handshakes coupled with hugs. We have created a culinary experience that is called Soul Food. Our brethren in the Caribbean have created Jamaican dishes that are healthy and delicious (and may in some instances be influenced by Mother Africa). The sixties brought us Black Pride which led to us wearing Dashikis (another transplant from Mother Africa). We also began wearing what some called Afros or Naturals. The 80s had us wearing what we labeled as "fade" hairstyles. These included Flat top fades and asymmetrical fades. The 90s came with the introduction of the Kente cloth pattern into our daily dress.

The point I am making is that we have created those things that fit neatly into what constitutes culture. However, we have some aspects of our culture that I think are overdue for evaluation in terms of looking to see if some of our cultural tendencies, accepted behavior and thoughts do more harm than good.

Speaking White

We must deal directly with our tendency to be disrespectful and insulting to other African people because they "talk white." What constitutes "talking white?" If we conclude that someone is "talking white" just because they can speak with clarity and have an extensive vocabulary, we are being short sighted. In America, English is presently the dominant language. A mastering of the spoken and written forms of English allows a person significantly more opportunities in this society than a person who is unable to express themselves clearly. Every aspect of life requires communication. Something this important should not be taken lightly. Furthermore, anyone who has enough wisdom to make communication mastery a priority is thinking clearly and intelligently. Certainly, we do not want to embrace a culture that has an opposition to intelligent life strategies, do we? Additionally, just because a person of African descent speaks a certain way does not mean that they have no interest in issues, problems or concerns that plague the Black community. In fact, our leaders and spokespersons will need to have this firm grasp of communication to be best prepared to articulate what it is that we need. Lastly, let us not judge our brethren simply by their speech. Instead judge people by what they do and not what they say or how it is said. Remember, the good book says you can judge a tree by the fruit it bears. In other words, people are best defined not simply by how they speak or dress. No, we must learn to judge people by their deeds, how they treat others and to what activities they donate their time. This is the most logical approach. Certainly, we all know people that speak "Black" and radiate a certain charisma. However, some of these same individuals indulge in harmful and predatory practices, so let's look beyond how people speak.

Honoring Gangster Lifestyles

For far too long the media has underrepresented the diversity of the Black experience. Too often the stereotypes about us focus solely on negative portrayals of who we are, how we act, what we desire, and how we treat one another. Over time, what happens, I think, is that we have started believing in these depictions of who we are. In fact, in many instances I think we have embraced certain images and lifestyles that are projected upon us that don't accurately reflect the variety of ways in which we live. This has been particularly harmful to our people who are products of difficult socio-economic upbringings. Yes, some of our people from resource strapped areas indulge in predatory behavior. The media has had a field day showing that side of our existence. But we need to be mindful that many of the behaviors (drug sells, pimping, theft, deception, etc.) that occurs in our financially challenged communities are attempts of survival in what many call the urban jungle. These behaviors are not innately attached to our DNA. We are prompted to act a certain way simply because we are trying to survive. Given different circumstances and opportunities, my urban brethren would in turn live differently. All one must do is look at the way suburban Blacks live versus urban Blacks. You will find that there is a vast difference. The difference in that behavior obviously, then, is the environment in which people have been raised.

But let's go back to what I touched upon in the previous paragraph. I spoke about us embracing images that others hold concerning us. One perception it seems that many people have is that a large percentage of Black people are criminally inclined. Unfortunately, many of us have accepted this portrayal of us. I, myself, have seen some rappers be dismissive of other rappers because they felt that the other rappers were too clean, not grimy enough. Some rappers have even been raised in the ideal family structure (two employed parents living with the child, nice neighborhood) and they still desire to be more gangster. This goes back to my belief that some of us start believing in these stereotypes about us. These rappers are a product of the seemingly ideal situation. Their behavior is not a product of their environment because the community from which they come has insulated them from certain experiences. So their desire to present themselves as more gangster seems to be more of an attempt to fit in, to live in accordance with what they deem to be acceptable "Black" conduct.

I have witnessed my sisters neglecting to consider dating certain guys because they were "too nice." Yes, I said "too nice." I did not say that the sister was opposed to giving the brother a look due to justifiable reasons. If she had said that the guy had a hygiene issue, I would understand. If she said she found out he was physically abusive to a previous female acquaintance, I would not bat an eye. Had she stated that he would not hold a job, and she needed someone she could build and grow with, no questions would be asked. However, she was only concerned with the man being "too nice." This happens too frequently in the Black community. Now with some of my sisters, this response or opposition to nice guys may be deeper than I intend to focus upon. Some would suggest past treatment received by the female who assumes this position is the reason she dislikes nice guys. Some would say that past life experiences have prompted her to unconsciously think that she deserves no better. Others would further argue that a damaged self-perception inspires her to seek dudes that are not nice. These are legitimate considerations, but I think these specific concerns should be addressed by a professional counselor who is trained to dig a little deeper to address the motivation behind such beliefs.

What I would like to emphasize is that it is obvious that past trauma can have a significant impact on our women's choices in males. However, if past negative experience is not the motivator for such decisions, we have to ask ourselves why it is that we make choices that may ultimately be harmful. Additionally, those of us who do not have to indulge in a gangster life because our basic needs have been met need to likewise ask ourselves why it is that we don't look at some other ways of presenting ourselves. The consequences of trying to be hard or more gangster are well documented: petty arguments that escalate into physical confrontations, poor life choices that are driven by bravado, being wounded, getting shot, prison time, and depleted guidance to the children of imprisoned or murdered parents, etc.

I think it is time we make a conscious effort to create a culture that helps us to progress collectively as a people. We can start by studying the cultural tendencies of our African and Native American Ancestors. I truly believe well-constructed cultural tendencies are in line with the educational, economic, political and spiritual needs of a people. For instance, a quick examination of both African and Native American culture shows that our ancestors understood names given to children have a shaping quality, so they chose names that had certain meanings so that the meanings associated with the names would help to mold the child as they grew. Dance and music have been identified as essential aspects of our ancestors' lifestyles. It seems that they understood that both activities elevate the spirit, thus increasing the likelihood that those involved were made to feel better. Furthermore, some would say that elevated spirits allow for a firmer connection with something bigger than us (the spirit realm?).

Our ancestors told us "it takes a village to raise a child." They seemed well aware that the nurturing of a child required participation from members of the community as well as the immediate family to help that child maximize his or her potential.

Let us now return to our initial concern that inspired this particular essay, the question of "what is Black?" I have concluded that those things that are innately "Black" are those practices indulged in by our ancestors prior to colonialism, slavery, and forced assimilation. If we can identify common behaviors exhibited by our ancestors on a global level, wherever they were on the planet, we can deduce with a degree of certainty that those self-expressions were consistent across the board because they are inherently part of the people.

We have already touched on how important naming ourselves was to our ancestors. We spoke briefly about their understanding of the need to collectively nurture a child. Other universal characteristics of Africans include a right brain dominant thinking style, taking a holistic approach to science, community ownership of property, word meanings or phrases corresponding to the context in which the word or phrase is used ("I got me a bad chick" could mean she is strikingly attractive), and the thinking that an individual's value is determined by what he or she contributes to humanity, not by what they own (Afrika, 1998).

Here are suggestions of additional things we could do. Let us consider creating community monitoring groups to keep our eyes open, being particularly focused on shielding our children and women from predatory and abusive individuals. Why not form study groups so that members of our subdivisions, blocks, cul-de-sacs, etc. will be actively engaged in the process of learning more about ourselves, our history and our gifts to the world. The creation of

African centered schools may give us more power to educate our children in ways that would increase the likelihood that a higher percentage of them would be prepared to maximize their potential, and thus be more prepared to be of assistance to our communities and humanity. We could organize trips to sites on the planet where African people have left documentation of their ingenuity (the pyramids in Kemet, cliff dwellings in Morocco, etc.). The list of possibilities is endless, but the point is this.

All of the cultural tendencies we identified are rooted in the elevation of African people. The same applies to the additional suggestions I provided. What does this tell us? I think it tells us that if we want to move forward we must first go back. If we want to identify what it is to be "Black," we need to find out what behaviors our ancestors indulged in before oppression and global domination forced us to assume tendencies that are not necessarily consistent with a people free to express themselves naturally. Let us examine what our ancestors were doing when we were building pyramids and creating science. I am not saying we need to discard all our cultural creations we have made in recent times. But I will say that when we find ourselves holding onto behaviors and thoughts that are harmful to us, those thoughts and behaviors need to be identified and removed. And I believe that when we finally start examining our historically correct cultural practices and embrace them, along with holding onto only those things that are beneficial to our people in the present, we will then be positioned to say in response to those behaviors and thoughts "that's Black."

Black History Month

This past January (2016), it was reported that Stacey Dash said in reference to Black people that "if we don't want segregation, then we have to get rid of channels like BET and the BET Awards and the Image Awards, where you're only awarded if you're black." She further stated that "there shouldn't be a Black History Month. We're Americans, period. That's it."

Well, let us address the latter statement first. Yes, we are Americans. As I stated before there is scientific evidence that proves that the first inhabitants of the Western Hemisphere were African people, some of whom subsequently mixed with later arriving Mongoloids to create what we call Native Americans (Imhotep, 2011), so our claim to be Americans is every bit as valid as any other ethnic group, if not more so. We never questioned that. Dash is comparing apples to oranges when she says our desire to have a Black History Month and our own stations and award ceremonies is synonymous with segregation. Please!

We have created Black History Month, BET, the BET Awards, and the Image Awards because we have been historically excluded in this country. Throughout the history of the American media, we have been treated purposely as if we did not exist unless some criminal act could be attached to us. All too often movies of the past have shown us as coons, mammies and dimwits. At some point a wise people will stop merely complaining about how they are being represented in the media and create their own vehicle by which they can be portrayed honestly and completely. BET is the result of this need. We could either continue to allow Europeans to present us in very limited and primarily negative ways, or we could muster up the vision, courage, and fortitude to create the forum by which we could address the need to show ourselves in ways that are more consistent with the diversity of Black life. This is why BET was created. Dash criticizing African people for creating BET is analogous to someone having a problem with a female that has been raped and now decides to learn martial arts or decides to obtain a permit to carry a concealed weapon. In both instances, we are blaming the victim for their natural and sensible response to attacks on their existence. No logical person - or sane one - should have any opposition to that.

Furthermore, the BET Awards and Image Awards were created because other award giving bodies have historically allowed politics to take a priority over artistic contribution when it comes time to hand out hardware. Deeper still, this society has often relegated our music to "jungle music" and in the process attempted to devalue what it is that we have created. This has been done with The Blues, Jazz, Rock and Roll, Funk and Rap. It is only later, after the powers-that-be have figured out that they can benefit financially from this "jungle music," do we see a real effort to market said music. This is not a gesture of sincerity. It is a matter of a few, privileged individuals with the proper connections simply saying let's make money off this form of expression if we can, regardless if we like it or not.

I wonder does Stacey know that segregation was created to minimize the forward progress of people of African descent. Does she know that along with segregation came a horrible court decision that was made into law? Has she heard of the Dred Scott decision, which said no person of

African descent could be a citizen in this country (Bennett, 1982)? That means that no person of African descent could have rights. This means that you could rape a Black woman, castrate a Black man, murder free Blacks and take their land, burn down their stores or businesses and suffer no consequences. None of this is speculation. This all has occurred time and again to our people. I would like to ask Stacey has she ever heard of the term Reconstruction, the period between the years 1865-1877 when Black Americans were supposedly granted their freedom. Surprisingly, despite centuries of oppression, African people began to prosper economically. Some had profitable businesses. Others had started to make a successful move into the world of politics. In response, the Ku Klux Klan (KKK) came into existence with the sole purpose of turning back the clock. They used every strategy possible-including mutilation and murder- to maintain the status quo (Bennett, 1982). In comparing BET, the BET Awards ceremony and the Image Awards to segregation, Stacey is implying (intentionally or not) that we want to violate the rights of people of European descent. She is insinuating that we want to dehumanize White Americans. Nothing could be further from the truth. We simply want fair treatment and accurate depictions of who we are. We also want to be awarded based on our merit. Sometimes you must create your own bodies and organizations to get that accomplished, and this is what we have done.

Benefits of Black History Month

Black History Month is an extension of Negro History Week, created by Carter G. Woodson, to speak to an obvious need, particularly in this country. The need we speak of is the need to acknowledge the global contributions of African people to history. Mr. Woodson recognized the obvious exclusion of African people and the things that they brought forth to humanity. He also was keenly aware that many things accomplished by people of African descent have been incorrectly attributed to Europeans. It is within this environment of exclusion that Negro History Week was formed.

What are the benefits of having a Black History Month? There are many benefits to be derived from its existence. The most obvious benefit is that having a Month assigned (February) to the study of African contributions provides us the opportunity to educate all ethnic groups about the contributions made by Africans. This accomplishes a few goals, one of which is that people are afforded an opportunity to have a more accurate understanding of history and how it has truly unfolded. This is true scholarship, and if we profess that we want a society - in fact a world - of truly informed people, we will allow history to be observed minus the politically fueled tendency to leave out the history of a select few. Secondly, whereas typical history classes have a damaging impact on the psyche and self-esteem of Black people, a more accurate telling of history can serve to amplify the pride of African people. This serves several purposes. When a people are constantly told (erroneously) that they have created nothing of historical significance, the natural human response is to remove oneself from this source of discomfort. So, when Blacks are told by our present educational institutions that we have only been slaves and entertainers, why would we be surprised that so many African youth have an opposition to school, an institution that systematically robs us of our self-worth by its biased presentation of history. The great Albert Einstein had this to say:

"Racial prejudice has unfortunately become an American tradition which is uncritically handed down from one generation to the next. The only remedies are enlightenment and education. This is a slow and painstaking process in which all right-thinking people should take part." (Kinnebrew, 2015).

What does this mean? I take it to mean that consciously misinforming people, both European and African, has negative consequences for both groups. In the case of Africans, I already discussed how consciously omitting our historical contributions affects our self-worth, but it impacts Europeans as well. First, it does them a disservice from an academic perspective, giving them faulty information which ultimately impairs their ability to speak from an informed place when it comes to forming remedies for social ills that plague Black communities. Yes, Black History must not only teach us about African contributions, but must also completely educate us all about the limitless obstacles that have been placed in the paths of African people. Far too many think our current conditions result from our innate inferiority and not the conscious effort of many to keep us in a perpetual state of servitude. This faulty presentation of information leads to bias, prejudice and arrogance. As stated by Einstein, such damaging thoughts can be eliminated by ensuring that everyone receives an accurate historical education.

Additionally, the same misunderstanding, bias and arrogance amassed by some Europeans resulting from our exclusion from history can cause them social problems. For example, a good friend of mine who is a Black acquaintance told me of the story of her childhood friend and an experience that he had at an institution of higher learning. Her childhood friend had always been an excellent student. In fact, he was my acquaintance's high school valedictorian. Much like my female acquaintance, he was of African descent. While in college, he happened to have a roommate who was of European descent. They become close friends and had no problems getting along. They had no history of arguments or disagreements. Then something happened that changed the nature of their relationship: They received their report cards indicating their respective academic performance. It seems that the young man of European descent did well and proudly boasted of his grade point average. His roommate, the childhood friend of my female acquaintance, likewise acknowledged his scores that he received. Well, it seems that the Black roommate's scores were higher than those of the White roommate. Unfortunately, the White roommate did not take this well. In fact, he developed an attitude in response to finding out that his Black roommate had exceeded him in terms of his academic scores. From this point forward, the relationship never quite recovered, and they reportedly never regained the rapport that they once shared.

What happened? Why did the White roommate respond so negatively to discovering that his Black roommate had scored higher than he? Is it possible that due to the incorrect telling of history that he had received, he had been deluded into thinking that Blacks were innately inferior, and thus incapable of outperforming him academically? Is it conceivable that he was unsettled by the fact that a member of an ethnic group that was closer to primates (as told by history and propagated through the media) could outperform him? What did this say about his intellect? How could he explain this to friends or family members who, like he, assumed that no Black could match his intellect. This is the inner turmoil that results from misrepresenting an entire ethnic group. Not only does it damage the group that is wrongly presented or excluded, it minimizes the understanding that we are all equal. If such an understanding had already existed, the White roommate may have had the necessary humility to concede that a Black could outperform him, while also understanding that it was not a negative reflection of his own talents or abilities, being that we are all the same.

Other benefits of telling a more accurate side of history, particularly acknowledging African contributions, is that Black students are more excited by history, knowing that people who looked like them have played a role in the progress of the human family. This same excitement could very well lead to Black students being more enthusiastic about history and learning in general. Perhaps this could lead to Black students being less disruptive in class. Remember in a previous essay we discussed, people act out when they have no means of saying "**I Am**" (I exist, hear me, I contribute, etc.). I believe that an awareness of one's ancestors' contributions will minimize those feelings of invisibility and allow the student to be more inclined to be calm and attentive. This benefits all the other students as well because the instructor will have fewer behavioral issues to deal with. Therefore, more time could be donated to teaching and less will be given to disciplinary concerns. Furthermore, Black students who are more excited about school and are less prone to be behavioral problems may begin to perform better in classes. This in turn increases the likelihood that these students are enhancing their chances for obtaining further education. This additional education, or skills acquisition, will improve young Blacks' chances of earning legal incomes, in the process making it easier to provide the economic foundation upon which stable family structures can exist. Can we talk about role models? Yes, Black history can inspire our young people to aspire to match the scientific and entrepreneurial achievements of those that came before. The awareness that other Africans created banks and department stores (Maggie L. Walker),pioneered blood plasma preservation (Dr. Charles Richard Drew),created the automatic traffic signal (Garrett A. Morgan), created over 300 ways to use a peanut (George Washington Carver), established four-year accredited colleges (Mary Jane McLeod Bethune) and boasted of entire towns controlled and run effectively by Africans (Black Wall Street) provides the real life examples to let our young people know that nothing is impossible because our ancestors have already achieved anything you can imagine. Finally, I believe that because of all the previous reasons I have stated, the potential for a stronger America will be a reality due to more African people fulfilling their human potential.

Is there still any reason to be opposed to having a Black History Month? I think not.

A Question of Age

This country, The United States of America, has an interesting relationship with age. Many people who are growing older are doing everything in their power to diminish the effects of advancing age, especially as it relates to physical appearance. Some have taken up exercise and dietary adjustments to try to slow down the aging process. Others have had plastic surgery to minimize the appearance of getting older. On the flip side, you have young people who are doing all that they can to seem older than they are. Some have obtained fake identifications. Others simply lie about their age because they may want to enter a party, attend a certain movie, or spend time with an older person of the opposite sex.

This society, when it comes to entertainment, puts a premium on youthfulness. It seems that the music industry is especially fond of young singers, dancers and bands. One argument I have heard forwarded as to why the music industry aggressively attempts to sign young artists is that studies indicate young people are more inclined to purchase music, and the young purchasers are more willing to buy music if the artists look more like them. I do not know if that is true or not, but commercially it does make sense to try to sign young people if there is a correlation between age and music sales.

My concern is that this country has no respect, in my opinion, for the normal maturation process. In indigenous cultures, elders are shown respect. Here in America that type of respect does not come often. We are all aware of the age discrimination that is practiced here, how trying to obtain employment after a certain age becomes terribly difficult, regardless of the skill set brought to the table by the mature person in question. Let there be a person of advanced age driving too slowly, and it is inevitable that the older person is going to be referred to as "grandpa" or "grandma."

Likewise, I have seen older people respond dismissively to the styles of dress, music, and habits of the youth. No, I am not saying we should accept the fashions, entertainment and activities of our young people without question. That is not a wise decision. What I am saying is that we were all young once and many of the styles of dress and music to which we gravitated annoyed our parents and older people in general. The key, I think, is to objectively analyze what the youth are doing. We should ask ourselves if the behaviors in which our young are participating have any damaging possibilities. If so, we are morally obligated to intervene and direct them on a better path.

But this is not directly my focus for this essay. I first wanted to highlight what I consider to be an issue that we take for granted. I have intended to demonstrate that age is a real concern in this country, and although we often do not consciously think about it, we do in fact have seemingly conditioned responses. What I think is a more reasonable practice is to identify the attributes–particularly the beneficial ones- associated with being young as well as the characteristics of being more mature (an elder); in doing so I hope to empower us to be more aware of the fact that both groups have something beneficial to offer to the other. Because of this awareness, maybe we can begin to become less insulting to one another and start becoming more appreciative of what each respective group provides.

Characteristics of Young People

1. Energy/Stamina
2. Athletic
3. Open minded
4. Receptive to Technology

Let's address the first characteristic of young people, energy/stamina. I had mentioned in the previous essay (What is "Black") that one of the things that we could consider would be to have monitoring groups in our communities to be assigned the responsibility of keeping their eyes open for predatory behavior in our neighborhoods. Our young men, nurtured with a sense of love for self and community, could work in conjunction with our elder men to serve as the "muscle" as the physical enforcers of this monitoring group. Furthermore, why not consider having a list made of young men, including their phone numbers, who would make themselves available to assist elders with things that their physical bodies struggle to do. There may be times when some of our elders who are in poor health may need their grass cut. Perhaps someone of advanced age needs their car washed. It may be a time when someone of a more mature status needs something moved or hauled, but the object is too heavy or cumbersome for them to manage. Keeping a list of young people to call to provide help in those moments might not be a bad idea. Yes, we would have to be respectful to the young people on the list, allowing them to schedule a time when they would do a certain physical task for an elder. Additionally, we should make sure that we can pay them something for their time and effort. But I think these are some of the ways we can benefit from the more youthful members of our communities.

Speaking of characteristic number two (athleticism) recalls an idea. Our young people seem to enjoy sports. It might not be a bad idea for more of us who have the time to do so to create local football teams, basketball teams, track teams, baseball/softball teams, soccer teams, tennis teams, etc. to provide an alternative means for our youth to expend their energy in ways other than getting involved in the street life. Many of our elders were themselves once athletes and still possess the understanding of how to play certain sports, so they would be in a good position to start these teams. The challenge comes when we are forced to acknowledge that some elders, though still possessing the mind for sports, may now be at a disadvantage when trying to physically demonstrate certain fundamental movements that are essential to each sport. This is where the athleticism of our young adults comes into play. There may be instances that kids that grew up around us ultimately played high school or college level sports. They may never have performed professionally, but they too possess the fundamental skills that could be passed along to our pre-teens and our teenagers. If these young adults worked in conjunction with the elders, it could be a lovely working relationship. The elders may possess the organizational skills, discipline and motivation to establish these sports teams. The young adults would be better prepared to demonstrate certain fundamental moves to the teens and pre-teens than elders who may now struggle with arthritis.

Many of our young people seem to demonstrate an open mindedness that exceeds that of more mature adults. This can be a positive quality if channeled properly. After all, the world is changing. I am not saying all change is good, and I think more times than not we will recognize when to disregard certain changes, especially when it appears these changes are for the worse. However, we too must acknowledge that people are creatures of habit (got that from Mavis Reid), and those habits are reinforced over time. So you find many times that people of a more advanced age are reluctant to consider doing things differently than they have always done them, and really, it only makes sense. Habits are part of our comfort zone, and most of us do not like to step outside of our comfort zone. Our more youthful citizens have not lived as long, so they have not had as many years to reinforce certain ways of thinking or doing things. Consequently, they often appear to be more flexible in considering different ways to accomplish ends. They often appear less burdened by changes. Also, I think that the more youthful segment of our population has not been subjected to the great number of years of social conditioning, so they seem often able to think outside the box. I think this is a huge talent to possess, and with the rapidly changing world in which we reside, I believe this skill will only become more needed.

Technology does not appear to be going away. Computers are more prevalent than ever. Everyone has cell phones. Texting has replaced phone calls as a means of sending brief and instantly received messages in a pretty non-intrusive manner. Many people have laptops so that they can do work on the go, or simply to access the internet as needed. Our youth seem to have little to no opposition to the newer technologies and newer means of communicating. Our elders, however, seem to be less than enthused about them. Many of them refuse to learn how to access the "contacts" section of their cell phones so that they may be able to record peoples' names, address, telephone numbers and email addresses. It is not uncommon, in fact, for many of our more mature adults to still document phone numbers and addresses in books. The problem with this is that there are times when you need someone's information or need to contact them, but you do not know the information by heart. What do you do when you are not home and are unable to lay your hands upon your phone book? I think this is where technology can be of assistance. I could go further, but at this point I want to now talk about some of the characteristics that our elders bring to the table.

Characteristics of Elders

1. Experience
2. Abstract Thought
3. Humility
4. Dispute Resolution
5. Aware of the Power of Propaganda

Experience provides an opportunity to grow in so many ways. Many times, we find people have certain talents or skills, and those abilities often result from the fact that this person demonstrating said skills has been living long enough to develop them. Life experience also affords elders the chance to recognize that to fail at any given thing is not the end of the world. Being elders, they have certainly lived long enough to have not met with success in all endeavors, yet they have lived to tell about it. Furthermore, experience alerts people to the fact that the very nature of the universe is cyclical. Situations or opportunities often present themselves more than once. Elders can convey to the youth that the key lesson to learn from failure is that another opportunity very similar to the one that just passed could very well come again. They can speak with confidence in telling the youth that the important thing to do is to examine why the objective was not met, not to give up, and to do whatever is necessary to improve in that particular thing that caused them to fall short. Elders have often learned that the key to success is to work smarter not harder.

Another attribute that is more likely to be associated with the more mature members of the population is the ability to think abstractly (Amen, 1990). The universe seems to have everything in perfect working order, so while younger people seem to possess the gift of physicality (energy, speed, stamina, flexibility, power, etc.), more mature individuals have developed the mental abilities to compensate for the loss of some of their physical gifts. Being able to comprehend elusive images, being able to digest philosophical concepts, being able to extract messages and meanings from film and science fiction seems to come more easily to the older members of our population. Is it no surprise that historically most of our priests, ministers and philosophers are mature in terms of biological years? It is simply a matter of people indulging in activities that come with the most ease for them at that time. Most 50-year-old men will struggle to dunk a basketball the way they once could, that is if they can still do so at all. Running that 40-yard dash in under 4.5 seconds is unlikely at 50 years of age. Those displays of physical power are for the youth. Our elders are blessed by the universe to be able to navigate the physical realm in a more cerebral manner. Let us be mindful of these different gifts and try to utilize them wisely.

A higher degree of humility seems to be another quality more often observed with elders. We spoke in earlier essays ("How to Avoid Unnecessary Competition" and "Humility") that humility is a state often achieved when we have accomplished certain goals, particularly if those accomplishments are noteworthy. Elders have lived longer. They have had more years to identify what they would like to do with their lives. They have had more time to ponder why it is that they exist. In pondering these types of questions, in pursuing their passions, they may have achieved certain goals that have elevated their sense of worth and achievement. Therefore, the need for elders to toot their own horns is less present. They may feel less of a need to say **"I Am"** because their accomplishments do that for them.

Another talent elders typically have in more abundance is the ability to resolve disputes in a peaceful way. I think a lot of this again is a product of experience, learning from previous interactions that responding with anger to anger just intensifies the collective rage of the parties involved. Elders in many instances may have learned firsthand that rage increases the likelihood that we will make emotional decisions, ones that may be both harmful and destructive in some way. With this recognition comes the awareness that more diplomatic tactics are often required. Furthermore, since more elders may have obtained a means of saying "**I Am,**" the need to be heard, to be right, to be the baddest is not nearly as much of a factor. So that ego driven behavior that will not allow some of the youth to tone down some of the aggression they exhibit in exchanges seems not to be as prevalent amongst our elders.

Finally, let us acknowledge that elders often appear to be more cognizant of the power of propaganda. This could be simply a product of having lived longer and seeing how the media time and again impacts tastes, styles of dress, art and culture in general. Maybe more elders have studied subliminal messages in college and books that they have come across. Perhaps they have observed their very own children being birthed from the womb with an apparent comfortability with themselves, only to watch them slowly become disenchanted with their own features because what is presented as attractive in the media does not coincide with their own features. Our younger members of the population may not be mindful of the power of the media to shape opinion and perception. They may not have been exposed yet to information that speaks of the influence of TV, literature and radio. Additionally, they still may possess a certain innocence about themselves because of their youthfulness, not yet coming to grips with the fact that some use the media for less than noble purposes.

Either way, these are some of the beneficial characteristics that I have observed to be connected to these groups, young people and elders. There may be more tendencies that I have not identified. However, my intention is not to attempt to establish the perfect list of attributes affiliated with each respective group. My goal is to bring into peoples' awareness the fact that both groups have something to offer. A dismissive attitude towards each other minimizes the depth of our connection. In doing so, we increase any division that already exists. When challenges arrive, and they will, it is best to have as large a pool of knowledge, skills and abilities as possible to enhance the chances to find the best solutions to life's questions. This is the most sensible approach to take.

"The Message"

This single song legitimized rap as an art form. Prior to the "Message," DJ's who often try to be impartial openly questioned if rap was anything more than gibberish and party music. All that changed after the "Message." Grand Master Flash and The Furious Five (featuring Melle Mel and Duke Bootee) obviously knew they had a monster on their hands. They could have very well named the song "Don't Push Me," "I'm Close to the Edge," "It's Like a Jungle Sometimes," or anything else in the hook which is the most memorable and identifiable part of the song. Instead, they chose a title that spoke to the essence of the song itself: "The Message." Everything about this song, from the production, to the lyrics, to the timing of its release (Reagan Era), to the world-weary delivery screams classic. This is arguably the most important song in the last 36 years.

You really must put this song in the proper historical context to understand its significance. Not only was it released during the Reagan years when there appeared to be a huge movement "right" in terms of political concerns, but the music of the times were nonpolitical. There were not a lot of people talking about universal love, racial pride or spiritual themes. It was more about getting your party or your "freak" on. It was like the world was asleep and that lack of consciousness was reflected in the music.

Remember, it had been 11 years since Marvin Gaye had released "What's Going On," ten years since the O'jays had released "Backstabbers," 10 years since the release of Curtis Mayfield's *Superfly*," 9 years since Earth, Wind and Fire's "Head to the Sky," 9 years since Stevie Wonder's

"*Innervsions*," 7 years since the Isley Brothers told us to "Fight the Power" and 6 years since the Isleys asked us "when will there be a harvest for the world." Obviously there was a different tone on the radio in 1982, perhaps in society in general. Maybe this different tone was reflected in the music of the times. Maybe we all thought that the American Dream had come true. It could be that we had been deluded into thinking that everything was fine, and everyone was doing ok. It is possible our artists thought there was no further need of speaking to societal issues, or had concluded that the listening public had lost interest in political or socially relevant songs. Perhaps the music industry itself had prompted the artists to tone down the political and social themes in their songs by not marketing those songs as fervently as they did the apolitical and socially non-relevant releases. Whatever the reason for the change in lyricism, know this: The world stopped and listened when Grandmaster Flash and the Furious Five dropped "The Message."

"Broken glass everywhere/ People pissin' on the stairs you know they just don't care/ I can't take the smell, can't take the noise/ Got no money to move out I guess I got no choice/ Rats in the front room. Roaches in the back/ Junkies in the alley with a baseball bat/ I tried to get away but I couldn't get far/ 'Cause a man with a tow truck repossessed my car/"

These were experiences that so many Americans could identify with in 1982, but you wouldn't know that poverty and urban decay existed if it was up to radio at the time to keep the people aware of what was really happening. Grand Master Flash and the Furious Five woke us all up, letting us know that it wasn't necessarily all good in the "hood." In the process they achieved the pinnacle of what all great songs do: entertain and enlighten.

But let's not stop there. We must acknowledge that in the same way that James Brown gave us the formula for the Funk so that the rest of the world would then know how to "get on the good foot," "The Message" served as the urban poetry with a social concern that opened the door for RUN-DMC to tell us about "Hard Times," and that sometimes "It's Like That." Whodini further confirmed rap's ability to speak to issues when they told us about "Friends" and the importance of "One Love." The Fat Boys told us about the tragic reality of being "in jail without no bail" in "Jail House Rap." KRS-ONE received the lyrical baton and blessed us with "My Philosophy," and Public Enemy continued the awareness onslaught with their version of "Fight the Power." Ed O.G and the Bulldogs pleaded with us to "Be a Father to Your Child." Nas asked the children to say "I Can," and informed us what he could do with "One Mic."

Sonically, "The Message" was just as impactful. The Furious Five's previous songs echoed the sound of what constituted Funk at the time. "The Message" sounded totally different from all they had done previously. This song was much more melancholy in tone. There was an evident monotone vocal delivery throughout the song (with the exception of the last verse) that smelled of despair. The funky horns were nowhere to be heard. The slap bass was absent. Now we hear a synthesized rhythm driving the groove as opposed to a bass guitar or a rhythm guitar. The music did not sound quite as organic. This gave the song a more futuristic sound, but it was a bleak future. The music itself implied a dark present may be morphing into even darker days to come.

This song along with Cameo's "Flirt," Prince's "1999," D-Train's "Keep On," and "You're the One for Me" were songs that helped change the sound of what Funk would be in the 80s.

So when we talk about great songs of the last 36 years, songs that changed the musical landscape, we must include "The Message." Not only did this song force subsequent rappers to step up their game lyrically, it forced a world skeptical of rap's potential impact to recognize that rap music could indeed be a force to be reckoned with. "The Message" informed us. "The Message" challenged us. "The Message" moved us, and we are all the better for it.

Purple Reign

April 21st, 2016 was another sad day for those of us who love music. The artist that the world had come to know as Prince departed this realm of existence. I think I can speak for my peers when I say that we all took Prince's transition hard. For one, there had been no warning. Some of us had heard that Prince's plane had recently made an emergency landing to get Prince the medical assistance he needed at the time because of him passing out and being non-responsive. This emergency landing happened six days before Prince died. I had not heard of the plane landing incident until after his passing. Nevertheless, I understood he seemed to be recuperating nicely, as indicated by the fact that he was performing live again shortly thereafter, even ensuring fans that he was okay by telling them to save their prayers.

Had we as fans been informed that Prince had been diagnosed, for instance, with terminal cancer several months before, we all could have developed some sort of mental preparation for the inevitable. Many of us would have been certain to make plans to attend his next performance, regardless of where it would take place. Some of us may have tried to attend one of Prince's live shows he often grants right there at Paisley Park- his living quarters, recording studio and performance facility. Unfortunately, it was not to be. We all received the painful news that Thursday that the man whose music has been with us from our teenage years up until now is no more. The suddenness and the finality of Prince's death has been an extremely bitter pill to swallow. His music is the soundtrack of my life. Pivotal moments in my life play back in my head while I can simultaneously hear his music serving as the backdrop to whatever I was going through at that time. How do you not feel the pain of his departure? How can you not feel like a part of you has died? Yes, his music will live on eternally, and for that I am thankful. However, the one main regret I have is never being afforded the chance to tell Prince directly how much he has electrified my soul with his music over the years. Here is my chance to do just that. I just pray I can present my words in such a way that they do his musical legacy justice.

He Never Diluted the Music

Let us go back to the early 80s, when Prince initially burst on the popular music scene. Yes, Prince had released his first solo project in 1978, but it was heard primarily on urban (Black) radio. Many initially thought that *1999* was Prince's first album because that is when MTV started playing his videos, thus exposing him to the pop audience for the first time. The reality is that *1999* was Prince's fifth musical release. Regardless, what became evident was the variety of different styles of music that he played. No artist since Sly and the Family Stone had combined so many genres unabashedly. The significance of this cannot be overstated. Putting this all in the proper historical context forces us to acknowledge the dramatic change this caused in the musical world.

Those of us old enough to remember can confirm that radio was highly segregated in 1982. The groups that dominated urban radio (Cameo, Slave, Confunkshun, The Barkays, Rick James, Shalamar, Parliament/Funkadelic Teddy Pendergrass, Peabo Bryson, etc.) were not known to our European peers. In fact, Rick James once threatened to sue MTV for not showing videos of Black artists, his in particular. In fairness to MTV, it started as a rock/pop video music showcase, and their playlist simply mirrored that of the segregated radio at the time. I am not sure racism or exclusion was the motivation. But this was the musical climate in 1982. The groups or artists that often were successful in crossing over changed the sound of their music to make it more palatable to the pop market's taste. Kool and the Gang, Ray Parker, Jr. and Lionel Ritchie were prime examples of artists who followed this blueprint to accomplish mainstream (pop) success. This often meant de-emphasizing the more African (Black) elements of the music so that it would be better received. Specifically, this meant that certain instruments were often given a lesser role in the music productions. Instruments like organs that elicit thoughts/feelings of gospel (The Black Church) were eliminated. The slap bass playing style created by Larry Graham was shelved for a finger playing technique. Horns were allowed if they were played melodically, but playing horns in a percussive style that was popular in funk music was not allowed. Furthermore, those artists that successfully crossed over emphasized those elements that the pop audience was better prepared to digest: melody and strings. If you were attempting to capture a bigger slice of the rock market, inclusion of the rock guitar playing style was a must, given the popularity at the time of groups like Loverboy, Def Leppard, AC/DC, VAN HALEN, etc. So what was happening is that a great deal of artists that started on urban radio and benefited from a Black base diluted their music to gain mainstream inclusion, and thus sell more units. Prince changed all of this.

1982 was the year when the music scene got a welcome kick in the rear. This was the year that Prince released the breathtaking *1999*. Yes, Prince had already begun combining different genres of music on *Dirty Mind* (1980), but on *Dirty Mind* his success was primarily that of critical praise from reviewers. *1999* gave Prince the commercial success, and the visibility, that had eluded him. Now the world would know him, and he never looked back.

What became evident on *1999* is that Prince made no effort to gain mainstream success by de-emphasizing certain elements of music as his peers had done. His music was always true to the African tradition. In saying that, I mean Prince's music on *1999* still was polyrhythmic. The funky basslines were still there ("Lady Cab Driver"). The soulful falsetto (passed down from The Temptations, The Delfonics, The Stylistics, The Temprees, Blue Magic, etc.) was still present. The nasty guitar lessons learned from Jimmy Nolen ("D.M.S.R.," "Lady Cab Driver") were quite evident. Yet, Prince combined these "Black" elements undiluted with rock styled guitar playing, New Wave keyboard sounds and rockabilly rhythms ("Delirious") to create a sonic stew that may have been unprecedented in popular music in the 20th century. What Prince did in the process was to continue to give up the funk as he always had to the fans who had followed his career for four albums, while earning new admirers by appealing to the rock and roll needs ("Little Red Corvette") of other music listeners. In doing so, Prince achieved what Kool and the Gang, Lionel Ritchie, Ray Parker, Jr. and others were unable to achieve; he expanded his visibility without compromising his musical roots or alienating his core base. In other words, many have turned their backs on us (the urban market) to be "large." Prince took us along for the ride, and we are forever indebted for the wonderful journey that it was.

Additionally, he helped bridge the gap that once existed in radio and video programs. Becoming one of the most recognized and successful artists in music led to Prince's music being heard by a more diverse crowd of listeners than were available on his first four albums. People who had never really listened to "Black" music (funk, soul, and gospel) were forced to do so when listening to Prince, oftentimes without even being mindful that that was indeed occurring. Being that Prince drew no obvious lines in his music distinguishing when he would navigate from one genre to the next, people found themselves listening to, and ultimately enjoying, styles and sounds that they would never have considered prior to their exposure to his music. In the process, he expanded the musical tastes of all who listened to his mesmerizing mixture. So now we have Black kids who grew up on the funk having listened to enough of Prince's rock inclusions that they are not turned off by the sounds of Stevie Nicks, Tom Petty and Pat Benatar. Similarly, White youth who had grown up on Kiss and others, being slyly introduced to Prince's funky world, were now becoming receptive to The Time, Sheila E., Ready for the World and other groups who emphasized a more rhythmic type of expression. In a nutshell, Prince was colossal in making pop radio more inclusive and more diverse in the sounds they played. This cannot be overstated. Can you imagine "The Glamorous Life" by Sheila E. being a top 10 pop song without Prince getting the world used to the nastiness of the funk? Speaking of nasty, I find it hard to believe pop radio would have embraced "Nasty" by Janet Jackson and allowed that to be in heavy rotation without Prince. The song is amazingly stinky, with an almost metallic funk quality to it. And when I say metallic, I do not mean that this song has heavy metal qualities to it. I mean to say that the drums sound as if the drummer is pounding on a steel object. There is nothing pop about it, but again, Prince had already infiltrated our homes and the airwaves with his sounds, getting us prepared for all the future musical stench that was to come. Thank God for his love of all sounds and refusal to play it safe.

Lyrical Prowess

My wife and I have always been Prince fans, and we have wonderful discussions about Prince as an artist and his vast talents. When discussing Prince, you will find that he has performed every aspect of musical expression at the highest level. You can talk about his virtuosity as a musician. You can find yourself being awed by his prolific musical output. One can speak about the varied clothing styles that he has displayed throughout the years. The live performances of Prince can be the centerpiece of a discussion for an extended period. It is for these reasons, I believe, that Prince has been the subject of many literary endeavors. Who knows, maybe in the future I may write an entire book totally focused on His Royal Badness. As for now, I would like to address Prince's brilliance as a song writer. This is just another component of his music that is stunning.

I think I first became aware that Prince was an advanced lyricist when I listened to the songs from *1999* from beginning to end. Whereas Prince had previously been rather risqué (to say the least) on his prior two albums, his references to things sexual now were treated more poetically. In the futuristic party anthem, "1999," Prince famously said, "If you don't wanna party, don't bother knocking on my door. I've got a lion in my pocket, and baby he's ready to roar!"

On albums past, Prince would have probably been a lot less tactful in stating the same thing. What seemed to be occurring is that Prince was starting to understand that speaking metaphorically requires more wit and thought. It comes off as being less offensive as well, even though the message is the same. Essentially, Prince was now demonstrating that he understood the significance of the old phrase: "It's not what you say, but how you say it."

This was further shown on the hit "Little Red Corvette." The title itself is a metaphor for a fast, sexually ravenous female that Prince had met. Unlike the past when Prince would have just talked about giving you "head...... 'til you're burning up," he spoke in subtle terms:

"Guess I should have closed my eyes when you drove me to the place where your horses run free/ but I felt a little ill when I saw all the pictures of the jockeys that were there before me/"

"Horses" was already referenced by Prince earlier in the song, letting us know that he was referring to the condom brand known as Trojans. Who rides on horses? Jockeys ride them, but again Prince was not speaking about jockeys per se. He was speaking about the previous lovers that he envisioned that this lady had been with. Prince could have said that he was feeling a bit uneasy thinking about all the lovers that preceded him with this female of interest in this song. Instead, Prince took the lyrical high road, telling us exactly what he meant without being crass. This was one of the first songs where we see His Royal Badness (Prince) being more tactful, and visual, with his lyrical presentation. On subsequent albums, he would raise the stakes further.

Where *1999* had made Prince a player in the mainstream market, *Purple Rain* made him an international superstar. One of the things that became obvious with the lead single, "When Doves Cry," is that Prince had again elevated his lyricism:

"Dig if you will the picture, of you and I engaged in a kiss/ The sweat of your body covers me. Can you, my darling, can you picture this/ Dream if you can a courtyard, an ocean of violets in bloom/ Animals strike curious poses. They feel the heat, the heat between me and you/"

Prince was now becoming more graphic with his words, referring to the "sweat "of his love interest that covers him. He further forces us to conjure images in our minds of a natural, peaceful place, one with "violets in bloom." Part of being a masterful storyteller is being specific with details so that the listener can not only hear the music, but in our minds because of the specificity, we can see the sweat soaked shirt caused by the friction of two lovers. We see the greenery and the accompanying natural vegetation. We are transported to the courtyard mentally, where we, too, see animals standing awkwardly, possibly because of their unfamiliarity of seeing humans at all, much less engaged in a passionate embrace. This is one of the goals when striving to present advanced lyrics. You want to make the listener see all the sights, smell all the odors, and hear all the sounds. Specific details assist in achieving this end. Prince apparently was starting to understand this well.

Another thing that we see is a transparency lyrically that we had not seen in *Dirty Mind* or *Controversy*. We had started to see it to some degree in *1999*, but we still were not sure when Prince was toying with us or being truthful. Most of songs on *Purple Rain* contained lyrics that seemed as if Prince was finally removing the veil of mystery that for so long had been a major aspect of his career. On "When Doves Cry" his pain is real, not manufactured:

"How can you just leave me standing, alone in a world that's so cold/ Maybe I'm just too demanding. Maybe I'm just like my father, too bold/ Maybe I'm just like my mother. She's never satisfied/ Why do we scream at each other. This is what it sounds like when doves cry/."

Prince has now decided that it is safe to let us in, maybe referring to his parents for the first time in his career. He is letting us know that he hurts like we do, that his interactions with his parents had left him troubled. By being so honest, we see his humanity. We feel his pain. With all his genius and eccentricity, we are more able to identify with him. In the process, we become closer to him, now understanding he is just like us. This is also part of being a strong lyricist: Writing in such a way that you establish a rapport with the listener, thus prompting them to want to listen that much more closely.

Finally, let us acknowledge how Prince used the metaphor of a dove crying to represent unhappiness. The dove is an international symbol of peace. If the dove cries, that means that peace is disturbed, that the very opposite of peace is the mood or feeling at the time. Prince did not say "this is what it feels like when I'm blue." He did not say "this is what it feels like when I am sad." He said, "This is what it sounds like when doves cry." You can't be more concise, graphic or poetic in expressing sadness.

Moving forward in time a few years, we find Prince had created another side group whose debut album he had written and produced. The name of the group was "The

Family." Prince had penned a lovely tune for them titled "Nothing Compares 2 U" (yes, the same single ultimately made famous by Sinead O'Connor years later). Here again we can observe another elevation in skills by Prince in song writing. Typically, when we tell people how long we have been doing something, we start with the largest description of time, followed by the next largest, and the next, with the smallest measure of time being the one mentioned last. For instance, if someone were to ask how long it's been that you have been married; most people would say something like 7 years, 2 months and three weeks. This is the usual way that we Americans speak when it comes to questions concerning the length of time we have been doing something. Prince, being ever desirous of a way to shock our ears, recognized this trend when it comes to speaking about time. Consequently, he figured out a formula to approach speaking of time in a way that was counter to what we had become accustomed.

The first line in the song "Nothing Compares 2 U" goes like this:

"It's been 7 hours and 13 days, since you took your love away."

Immediately our ears perked up. We instantly recognized that the smaller length of time (hours) had been used before the larger length of time (days). Right from the very beginning Prince had achieved what all artists strive to do with the opening line of a song, command your attention. With that simple reversal of descriptors of time, Prince also gave the song, by way of the opening lyrics, a more poetic and distinguished sound. The singer of the song sounds more sophisticated by having the means to express a very simple idea in a way that most of us never ever consider. In some ways, it is analogous to someone saying "process" (proh-cess) instead of saying "prah-cess," which is how most Americans would say it. The former pronunciation would be more likely to be uttered by someone of British descent. We may or may not be aware of it, but we Americans usually find the British pronunciation more satisfying than ours, possibly because it is foreign to us, therefore projecting an almost exotic flair when pronounced in the way that is more associated with the British. By making the simple reversal in the descriptions in time, Prince was able to project that same type of exotic lyrical beauty.

None of this was apparently lost on Dallas Austin, who wrote the Grammy award winning "Creep" for the female trio T.L.C. The opening line for "Creep" says:

"The 22nd of loneliness, and we've been through so many things."

Here we find the basic adjustment of how we speak to time being a pivotal part of the opening line. Much like "Nothing Compares 2 U," the initial line to "Creep" stuns us on an auditory level. We were more used to people saying something like, "I have been alone for 22 days." Another common approach at the time would have been to say something to the effect of, "My man left me 22 days ago." Those were typical ways to express the experience. Dallas Austin, being a fan of Prince, had obviously been struck by the beauty and poetry of the opening line of "Nothing Compares 2 U," so much so that he borrowed the technique, and I say good for him. They say that the greatest form of flattery is imitation, so I am sure Prince was flattered when he heard the song, knowing his musical innovations were being observed and continued. However, Prince's impact did not end there.

T.L.C.'s second single, "Waterfalls," was an even bigger smash. I could talk about the musical elements Organized Noize used for "Waterfalls" that were obviously Prince influenced, such as the lovely horns that were reminiscent of how Prince's horns sounded and were arranged on "Slow Love" from *Sign 'o the Times*. The wah wah guitar brings to mind "Electric Chair" from the *Batman* soundtrack. However, the focus here is Prince's lyrical impact, so let's stay on course.

The hook to "Waterfalls" goes this way:

"*Don't go chasing waterfalls/ Please stick to the rivers and the lakes that you're used to. I know that you're gonna have it your way or nothing at all/ But I think you're moving too fast*"

Much like Prince's approach on "Little Red Corvette," T.L.C. speaks metaphorically, essentially informing the protagonist that the grass is not always greener on the other side.

Sign 'o the Times is regarded by many as Prince's greatest collection of music. I agree with that assessment. I would continue in saying that the album could very well be his strongest collection of lyrics also. Songs like "Strange Relationship" and "I Could Never Take the Place of Your Man" reflect an honesty, self-awareness and a transparency that makes the listener feel as if Prince is speaking directly to them, giving them a direct line to who he is, including all his imperfections and shortcomings. "Adore" possesses, in my opinion, arguably the single greatest chorus ever written:

"Until the end of time, I'll be there for you/ You own my heart and mind, truly I adore you/ If God one day struck me blind, your beauty I'd still see/ Love's too weak to define, just what you mean to me/"

Now let's think about that chorus for a second. Prince is saying that his affection is so strong that as long as the universe exists, the female object of his desire will be loved by him. He did not say "until he is old and grey." He did not say "until his dying day." He made reference to the end of time, but time as we know it never ceases, so what he is saying is that the strength of his love will transcend time, dimensions, reincarnations and what other forms of existence you can imagine, but he did not stop there. He continues by acknowledging that the beauty possessed by the object of his desire is not merely physical, that if his physical vision was taken away, he would still be keenly aware of her loveliness. Lastly, he confirms the power of his feelings by saying "love's too weak to define, just what you mean to me." Love is one of the most powerful energies in the universe. It inspires us to sacrifice our very lives for others. It prompts us to go to jobs that damage our spirit because we know the income from said job provides financial stability for ourselves and our families. It is one of the energies that often precedes physical intimacy, the act that ultimately allows for the human race to be perpetuated. In saying "love's too weak to define just what you mean to me," Prince is in a nutshell saying that he is incapable of finding the words strong enough to capture the feelings that he holds for this particular lady. Isn't that as profound a statement as any lyricist can make? I would say yes.

Last but not least, we must touch upon the outstanding "If I Was Your Girlfriend." Here Prince wants to alert the female object of his desire that he wants a relationship that is based on more than the typical male and female interactions. So often, women have lovers (husbands or boyfriends), but they reserve certain exchanges only for their female friends. Prince is aware of this, and envies how his lady confides in her girlfriends in ways that she will not share with him, so he asks the question:

"If I was your girlfriend, would you remember to tell me all the things you forgot when I was your man?"

When Prince's love interest establishes these borders on information exchange, Prince seems to conclude that his lady views him primarily as a romantic partner. He wants to be her best friend so that they can share the little things that she shares with her girlfriends. In Prince's view, it is the little things that mean the most. This is conveyed when Prince sings:

"If I was your girlfriend, would you let me dress you, I mean help you pick out your clothes before we go out/ Not that you're helpless, but sometimes those are the things that being in love's about."

What Prince has done so well in this song is demonstrate his powers of empathy, in terms of placing himself in his partner's shoes and viewing how she perceives the nature of her relationship with her man (Prince) and how it differs from the nature of relationships she has with her girlfriends. Prince does not want to be just one aspect of her life. He wants to be her everything, as confirmed by one of his final statements in the song:

"Maybe you think I am being a little self-centered, but I want to be all of the things you are to me."

In concluding the song this way, Prince is saying in a concise way that his lady is his all, his world. He simply wants to reciprocate. This is truly a fitting way to end such a thought provoking and insightful song.

Spiritual Significance

One of the ironies concerning Prince is that he initially presented himself as someone who loved the pleasures of the flesh to an extreme degree. That is not necessarily a bad thing, but in time it became apparent that Prince was extremely driven by spiritual matters. It appears that Prince understood the idea of purpose, that humans are manifested in flesh not simply to work most of one's life for someone else, retire (hopefully) one day, and ultimately perish. Evidence of the awareness Prince had of purpose can be extracted from his decision he made as a teenager. Many of his peers state that Prince once loved basketball and music equally, but he realized that to be great at one of the two, the other had to take on a secondary role. With this understanding clearly in mind, he threw himself fully into music. And certainly I must concede that only being 5'2 helped to make the decision for him, but the point is that even as a teen he recognized choices must be made in terms of why we are here and what we are more inclined to be successful doing. Additionally, Sheila E. has stated that one of the reasons that Prince worked so hard is that he wanted to continue to take us higher through the music. That is purpose-identifying your reason for being and doing all that you can to ensure that you fulfill that. After all, Oprah Winfrey once said on one of her shows that our reason for being is "to serve." Obviously "serving" and "purpose" are often one and the same. Prince grasped this truth early on.

But let's get a little deeper with this concept of purpose as it relates to Prince. I have concluded that he was incarnated to touch us through music. Let us look at his upbringing in Minneapolis and observe how factors seemed to conspire to move him towards a career in music.

We all know that Prince's father, John, was a jazz pianist and had his own band. We are additionally aware that Prince's mother (Mattie Shaw) was a vocalist with John's band. In having a child together, they assured that their descendent would be genetically predisposed to have an ear for music, much like the father. Furthermore, jazz musicians are known for their compulsive commitment to their craft, which often leads to wonderful musicianship, as evidenced by the fact that jazz musicians are often considered some of the premiere technicians that exist. Prince could have very well inherited this same type of commitment to musical perfection which led to him being a virtuoso on several instruments. Vocally, Prince benefited genetically from a vocally gifted mother, which gave him the vocal foundation to be one of the most gifted singers of the last 38 years.

Additionally, it has been said that Prince and his father did not always have a harmonious relationship. In fact, it is documented that John kicked a young Prince out of the house because Prince was caught being intimate with a girl. It was primarily because of the lack of peace that Prince felt at home that prompted him to move in with a school peer and friend of his, Andre Cymone. As fate would have it, Andre was also musically inclined, already demonstrating talents on the horns, bass and guitar. Prince lived with Andre for years, and it seems that Prince could not only jam with Andre pretty much whenever they desired, but legend has it that Prince lived in the basement where he could turn down the volume on his guitar and play when the spirit moved him. This gave him the space, freedom and opportunity to play for extended periods of time which ultimately led to the dexterity for which Prince became known.

Furthermore, Minneapolis during Prince's formative years was not a mecca for black culture. In fact, Prince has said himself that it was a challenge to even hear black radio stations. This truth, which could initially be perceived as a setback, benefited Prince and Andre. By being in a city that was not "black," those things "white" were made more available. For example, Prince and Andre, though challenged to find a means to hear urban radio, had free access to other musical sounds like rock and roll. This same exposure to rock during Prince's and Andre's formative years helped them to develop a natural appreciation for the genre which allowed them to effortlessly play it along with the other genres they would master. Prince's incorporation of rock stylings into his music never sounded forced, and I believe the exposure to it during his formative years played a role in that. Again we see how life factors seem to be conspiring to make Prince the artist that he was. Can we say **destiny**?

Minneapolis lacking black culture may have benefited Prince in other ways also. Let us consider that it is not uncommon for many youths who find it difficult to find happiness at home to seek it in the streets. This can lead to involvement with gangs as a means of developing a sense of belonging. It can lead to drug use as a means of escaping one's discomfort by numbing the emotional pain. It is not uncommon for youth to become prematurely sexual, because they may find comfort in someone's embrace. Yes, Prince had music to insulate him from his unhappiness. We have touched on this previously, but I want to mention that Minneapolis also lacked some of the other temptations that other cities had. Sure, Minneapolis had drugs, but the point I want to emphasize is that Minneapolis lacked the tantalizing street distractions that may have been more prevalent had Prince grown up in Chicago, Los Angeles, New York or The District of Columbia. I think this was one other factor working in Prince's behalf that helped him and Andre live the life of isolation that is necessary for advanced musical study and practice.

Lastly, I want to take a quote from Prince's own mouth. On more than one occasion I read or heard Prince audibly say that "music should be free." I think Prince felt that music was a gift from the universe. I believe Prince conceived of music as a universal language. After all, what we call music is nothing but vibrations generated by the striking of percussive instruments, the strumming of the guitars and basses, the sounding of piano chords, etc. It has been said that everything that exists is nothing but vibrations, that the different vibrational frequency of objects provides the perceived physical differences. I am certain that Prince had this awareness. I think that Prince felt that we have no right spiritually to put a price on vibrations. They preceded man's existence and will continue long after we no longer exist as physical beings. I have speculated from my studies of his views that this would be consistent with how he thought of music.

Let us go further as we discuss Prince's spiritual aspects that he brought to the table. Prince established long ago a desire to combine the sacred and the secular. A prime example of the attempt to mesh the two can be observed by listening to the *Purple Rain* album. In the song "Darling Nikki" Prince is singing about a female he met in a hotel lobby "masturbating with a magazine." This song created quite an uproar at the time, inspiring some to perhaps conclude that Prince was more concerned with matters of the flesh than anything else. Of course this conclusion was not hard to make considering that *Dirty Mind* (which preceded *Purple Rain* by some years) up until that point was probably one of the most blatantly sexual collections of music ever released. "Darling Nikki," to some, simply confirmed that Prince was nasty. But on the same album with "Darling Nikki," Prince included another song that was just as joyous musically as "Darling Nikki" was stripped down. This song further was just as spiritual lyrically as "Darling Nikki" was lewd. Obviously the song I am referring to is "I Would Die 4 U." Some of the lyrics are as follows:

"I'm not a woman. I'm not a man/ I am something that you'll never understand/ I'll never beat you. I'll never lie/ If you're evil I'll forgive you by and by/"

Prince goes on to sing in the chorus:

"U- I would die for you"

Obviously this song was inspired by spiritual teachings, probably the concept of Jesus as given to us by The Bible.

Jesus was known to forgive. Jesus' humility and meekness gave him a presence that was unlike other humans. This is the image Prince was trying to convey with "I Would Die 4 U." On this album it was becoming evident that Prince strove to combine the spiritual with the secular. Another example of his attempt to do this can be extracted from the ballad "Adore" from *Sign o' the Times*. In the song Prince sings:

"*When we be making love, I only hear the sounds/.... Heavenly angels, crying up above, tears of joy pouring down/*

I believe this was Prince trying to merge the pleasures of physical intimacy along with a divine experience, one not frowned upon by heavenly beings-angels.

Further examples of Prince attempting to combine the spiritual with the secular can be shown when we reflect upon the symbol that has come to be associated with the man. The symbol is said to be a merger of the astrological symbol for Mars (which represents men) and the astrological symbol for Venus (which represents females). It has been said that Prince wanted to combine the two, and image makers associated with Prince at the time were assigned the responsibility of combining the two images in a way that would be representative of Prince. This merging of the two principles, male and female, deserve some discussion, as this effort to bring into existence a sort of synthesis has always been a Prince tendency.

Yes, Prince's music has always been a hybrid of different genres. This is one example of a perpetual desire to synthesize elements. We have additionally highlighted lyrics that demonstrate this desire. But it seems that in terms of image, Prince really wanted to merge the male and female principles. Much like the concept of the yin and the yang derived from Taoism where the yang represents the male principle and the yin represented the female principle, there seemed to be an ever-present desire by Prince to make this concept a part of who he was. These seemingly opposite principles also represent day and night, positive and negative, heaven and earth, active and passive, and fire and water. There appeared to be an effort to not only have this synthesis be associated with himself, but he at times appeared to want to embody the concept of opposites (balance) that has been a spiritual concept for hundreds –perhaps thousands - of years. So instead of simply borrowing the image of the yin and yang that is widely recognized, Prince had his own symbol created that essentially projected the same idea. Remember this is Prince that we are talking about. To simply borrow an image that has existed for so long would be too simple for him. Much like the music Prince gave us that challenged us and forced us to grow with him, to adopt an already widely recognized symbol would be too easy. Prince always seemed to favor a good challenge. In the process, he challenged us as well.

Lastly, let us think about how Prince often dressed. He often wore eyeliner, and he straightened his hair. He has worn ruffled shirts and high heeled shoes. His songs often contained moments where Prince vocalized high pitched squeals. Some perceived these moments as feminine gestures. However, Prince was also known for his baritone speaking voice that has left many a female swooning. Additionally, any questions about Prince's sexuality must be put to rest when you consider the long list of beautiful women he romanced. In a way it seems that Prince not only embraced the concept of opposites (balance) on a theoretical level, but sometimes it appears his existence was a real-life effort to be that balance. After all, when there is imbalance there is chaos. Where there is balance, there is peace. I think Prince strove to help make balance, and thus peace, more real by being the very thing he wanted the world to be.

I could go on for an additional twenty pages just speaking about this wonderfully complex being we came to know as Prince, but that is not really the idea behind this series of essays. I would like to say that no artist has ever taken me higher so consistently and for such a sustained period of time. His departure has left a hole in my soul that perhaps only time will heal. To say he will be missed by me and millions on the planet is an understatement. Time will only confirm how significant he was to us all.

Rest well, my brother.

Prince and Rap Music

(The following essay started as a response to a friend on Facebook. Prince had recently made his transition to the spirit realm. Many fans used Facebook as a means to publicize their sadness in having to deal with the departure of the artist known as Prince. This particular friend made it obvious that he had never been a fan of Prince, thought Prince was "weird," and believed that Prince did not like rap music. He especially found it troubling to show love to Prince because he (the friend) is a rapper. I initially had determined that I would do my best to take my friend's views in and not respond. After further thought and consultation with my wife, I determined that the love Prince had shown through music justified that I bring some additional understanding to the table in terms of some of the things that Prince had done with regard to Rap Music. Here is what I stated):

My dear brother, I respect your feelings that you have about the recently transitioned artist known as Prince. I also understand how Prince's eccentric tendencies could be interpreted as weird. However, you mentioned that he did not like rap, nor did he like rappers sampling his music. Those two characteristics of Prince (not liking rap music or liking people sampling his music) deserve some clarification.

Prince did not dislike rap, or the essence of urban poetry. He has himself incorporated rap several times throughout his career into his music, even in the face of opposition to the inclusion of it from his fan base. As far back as 1983, Prince had a song titled "Irresistible Bitch" that was a B-side single. Here was his first, but certainly not his last, incorporation of hip hop elements into his music. Listen to his hit "Alphabet Street" and notice that at the latter part of the song, his background vocalist and dancer, Cat, is heard performing rap. Observe the "Batdance" video when time permits, and you will hear and see Prince scratching (a hip hop technique) in the video. In 1991, Prince released *Diamonds and Pearls.* On this cd, Prince introduced the world to Tony M, his in-house rapper, a full-fledged member of the New Power Generation, Prince's band at the time. You can hear Tony M. being featured on the songs "Daddy Pop," "Jughead," "Push," and "Live for Love." Prince even spits on some of the songs, and his timing as a rap vocalist was just as impeccable as his rhythm on the bass or guitar. 1992 was the year that Prince gave us the "Symbol" album. Here Prince really showed his appreciation of the contribution that rap had made to music. The first single, "My Name is Prince" includes scratching, a drum pattern that was inspired by the drum patterns of early 90s rap music and a rap delivery by Prince himself. "Sexy Motherf----r "showcases Prince combining Funk, Blues and Jazz with a rapping/spoken word verbal delivery. "The Flow" is a straight rap/funk workout. There is NO singing. Prince starts the first verse by responding to what he deems to be disrespect from an ill-informed journalist. Tony M. picks up the lyrical baton from Prince and continues the rap onslaught. "7" also includes a drum pattern that was consistent with what was occurring in rap music in the early 90s. Additionally, he samples "Tramp," the same single that had been wonderfully sampled by Salt-N-Pepa in the 80s. Listen closely to the entire "Symbol" album. It is very much a hip hop album, as there is scratching throughout the entire cd and very forceful drumming which any emcee at that time would have loved to be featured upon.

I know it appears that Prince did not like rap because he was opposed to rappers sampling his music. But the fact is that Prince was not crazy about ANYONE doing his music, regardless of the genre. But he was particularly concerned about allowing rappers to use his music because Prince felt too many rappers would be inclined to use his music to utter misogynistic lyrics. He also was concerned about the excessive gangster music that was taking place at the time, and he did not want his music to be part of any movement that would be harmful in any way.

Lastly, Prince has embraced other rappers enthusiastically throughout his career. It is documented that he was quite smitten with Salt of Salt-N-Pepa. Eve was featured on a single from *Rave Un2 the Joy Fantastic*. Prince has worked with Q-Tip and Chuck D. He has performed on stage with Doug E. Fresh. Both Common and Kendrick Lamar have been invited with open arms to Paisley Park, and Prince himself has gone on record as saying that he bumped Lauryn Hill's debut solo project so much that he "wore it out." One more thing, Prince, along with D'Angelo, were two of the biggest Soul artists to publicly embrace the political rap group Dead Prez. I understand that Dead Prez has opened for D'Angelo on stage before. Prince, in the meantime, went public with his admiration for the skills and lyrical content of Dead Prez, telling all that would listen that they were a duo that the world needed to hear.

Yes, there are a lot of misconceptions held about Prince. I once held a few myself, but extensive study of his catalog and contributions opened my eyes. He has taken me higher so many times, touched my soul so deeply. I felt morally obligated to try to clear up any misunderstandings my friends may have of him.

BET Scored a Home Run with Prince Tribute

Love is often an overused word. I think that it is often misunderstood as well, in terms of what it really means. Yes, love is how someone makes you feel, whether it is romantic love or more like a family vibe that you feel when thinking about someone or when you are in that person's company. However, I would like to stress that I think that "love" is an action word. It is something that you do. I am not sure how much time passed between Prince's transition and the showing of the Billboards Award ceremony that had Madonna paying tribute to Prince, so I am not sure how much time the people associated with Billboard Awards were provided to obtain an act or acts to pay homage to our wonderful Prince. I do remember thinking even then that with the time that they had that a better choice than Madonna could have been made. It is not that I necessarily thought little of Madonna as an entertainer. I just was not confident she alone possessed the vocal talent and instrumental skill to do Prince justice by herself. My wife suggested that many other artists should be pulled in to pay tribute, particularly those that were directly influenced by Prince or had come directly from his camp. This would have maybe given the Billboard's tribute to Prince more balance. Billboard should have considered this option. They were far too quick to settle on Madonna's contribution alone. Furthermore, Linda Perry attempted, feebly, to justify why artists like Chaka Khan, The Time and Sheila E. were not invited to perform, saying in a nutshell that those artists were no longer "relevant."

"Relevant?" Is this an opportunity to pay homage to Prince or an opportunity to get the most recognizable artists so as to increase viewing "numbers?" Perhaps we again have seen an example where the concern for the "bottom line" trumps the need to do the right thing, or in this instance trumps the opportunity to SHOW love. You show love, in this case, by contacting the artist(s) who are best equipped vocally, musically and energetically to best simulate what Prince has done in his career, and thus pay homage to his elevated artistry and musical contributions. You taker the extra time to make a list of the artists who are best prepared to bring to mind the spirit of Prince on stage. You take the extra time because Prince deserves that. Did he not bare his soul in song? Did he not put on some of the most dynamic live performances of our generation? Did he not expand the definition of popular music by constantly pushing the envelope? Did he not create a new sound that helped birth other popular artists (The Time, Vanity Six, Apollonia Six, Morris Day, Jesse Johnson, Sheila E., Ready for the World, The Family, Maserati, Jimmy Jam and Terry Lewis, Janet Jackson, Cherrelle, Alexander O'Neal, Terence Trent D'Arby, D'Angelo, The Jets, etc.)? Did he not give all that he had until he passed to the next realm? He most certainly did, and he did it because he loved us so. The Billboards Award show had a moral obligation to return the love and failed to reciprocate. Shame on them. BET, on the other hand, demonstrated love by enlisting those artists who knew Prince's music and costumes, and possessed both the vocal talent and skills as instrumentalists to imitate him and inspire a new generation to understand his unmatched power and influence. In doing so, they may have inspired the next generation to study Prince's massive catalog. Perhaps younger, aspiring artists will start playing live instruments because of this exposure to Prince's sound and his catalog. And if this happens, maybe the future of popular music will not be as dismal as it currently is. This is the impact of TRUE LOVE.

Thanks, BET. You got it right.

>Signed,

>*Afi Makalani*

Love, Family, Community and Purpose

Often, I have wondered what things are the most meaningful. I have thought long to determine what life is for, why we have come into being. I have asked myself time and again, "What are the most important things we could do?" What lesson or lessons are most important for us as humans to learn? After much study, prayer, meditation, personal observation and introspection, I have determined that the things that mean the most are love, family, community and purpose. My goal with this next essay is to attempt to show how these four things should dominate and direct our lives. Additionally, I will endeavor to demonstrate how these four things are interrelated.

Love

We touched on love lightly in the previous essay about BET and Prince. Love is complicated and can mean many things. However, one characteristic that I think absolutely must be associated with love is the unconditional expression of it. I think love means that you can demonstrate the ability to do for others without necessarily desiring anything in return. This obviously is what we mean when we use the term "unconditional love." I think another example of love is to have feelings of affection for someone that does not require that that person be flawless for those feelings to continue. I am of the thinking that if we only love people when their conduct is perfect, or in line with our desires, then this would fit within the category of conditional love and is not true love. Humans by nature are imperfect. We all make mistakes and will continue to do so until the Most High calls us home. If we only love individuals that exhibit perfection, we will never love anyone, because no man or woman can live up to that unrealistic expectation.

Love is about creating a place of emotional refuge- being that someone that an associate can confide in knowing that exchange of information will go no further. Being loving is being mindful of the fact that love is a higher vibrating energy and elevates the spirits of all that receives this energy. People showered with this affection in turn tend to interact with others in a warmer, more humane manner. I think many of us love family members or blood relatives, but our love discontinues there. For example, recall the instances that you may have been really annoyed with family members, but the exchange never elevated to the status of a physical confrontation. You may have even been so disenchanted with the family member in question that you did not interact with them for some time, but physical blows never took place. What held you back in those instances? Had you engaged in such a heated exchange with someone on the street, maybe even a friend, a physical fight may have ensued. Could it be that the unconditional LOVE that you had for the family member doused your hostility to the extent where you could walk away from the exchange with no physical interaction taking place? I think this is certainly a possibility. Just imagine if the human race evolved to the point where we truly loved all of humanity unconditionally, with no regard to ethnicity or physical appearance. How would this impact global relations? I know I am simplifying things a bit. Certainly economics and politics, which often conspire together, must be discussed when speaking of peace. But love is something that needs to be established early in life, preferably at home. The family is the nucleus, the first collection of people with whom we interact. It is important that families strive to make love for ALL of humanity a priority. At some point everyone in the family will leave the confines of the home and be required to interact with the world. It is time that the immediate family should start making it a priority to stress that while we may have minor differences, they are mostly physical, and our similarities far outweigh the superficial differences that we often give too much value.

Finally, I think it is important that we understand the significance of loving oneself and how that self-love works with regard to how we interact with others. It has been said before that to love others you must first love yourself. I, along with the current reader of this essay, have certainly heard this statement on at least one occasion. I am not sure I have heard anyone flesh the statement out, though, and explain specifically how this may work. Allow me to add my two cents worth at this point.

Yes, I think it is ideal to love oneself before claiming to love someone else. However, the question arises, "How does one learn to love him or herself in this often harsh, critical and exploitive world in which we reside?" I would suggest those of you reading this book study the earlier essay titled "How to Avoid Unnecessary Competition," especially the portion that discusses the method for developing a means to say "I am." I think this is a good place to start. Now, let's analyze what it means when we do not love ourselves in terms of how it may prompt us to interact with others.

When we do not love ourselves, we often operate from a place of perceived lack: We think we are not smart enough. We think that we are physically unappealing. We believe that we do not have the proper political connections. We feel we lack the necessary mobility or transportation. We think we do not have enough money, etc. What potentially happens when we have these perceptions (which are not always accurate), is that we can find ourselves dealing with others from a place of need. For example, a female may think that she is not attractive enough to catch the attention of members of the opposite sex. What she may be inspired to do is to unconsciously associate with other females who she thinks are considered by society to be less attractive. Being that so much of what we perceive is relative in nature, the thought that one's own physical attractiveness can be amplified by being surrounded by others who society deems less appealing is certainly a very real possibility. Unfortunately, the other females in this circle may believe that the relationship is based upon something of a higher nature like mutual concern, caring and sisterhood when it is not. This is one example of what can happen when we operate from a place of perceived lack.

Consider what may occur when our perception is that we do not have the necessary mobility to achieve certain objectives, but someone we know has a reliable vehicle. It is very possible that our desire to go certain places to achieve certain goals inspires us to connect with those individuals or that person that has that means of transportation we require. Again, we have an instance where the relationship is not necessarily as balanced as it should be. The perceived lack that we spoke of previously is, in this situation, having a significant impact on one person's desire to form a relationship. This could be a problem. The reason for me saying this is very simple. What happens when the person with the transportation stops being accommodating when it comes to providing rides for those that do not have mobility? What happens when the person with money discontinues providing financial assistance? What happens when the female concludes that her girlfriend only wanted to be seen in public with her to appear more appealing, but can't seem to find the time to come by to simply say hello and spend some quality time with her? This could be the point at which the relationship turns sour. Perhaps the relationship is terminated because one individual starts feeling exploited. The individual with the perceived lack may become unpleasant or angry because their need is being denied. The individual that feels used comes away emotionally wounded because they believed that the other person in question formed a bond with them that was meaningful, only to conclude that it was a one-sided relationship the entire time. This is why so many people are guarded and aloof. They have been mistreated in the past when they attempted to have sincere connections with others. Those of us who claim to want a better world need to reexamine how we treat the friendships afforded to us by others. Our mistreatment of them may cause some to put up emotional boundaries. These people may in turn decide it is better not to provide future assistance to anyone, even those individuals who are not exploitive and are truly in need of a helping hand. We have the power to improve our world as individuals by being honest and fair with those with whom we interact. Loving ourselves first is a step in the right direction.

Family

As I mentioned earlier, family is the first circle of people with whom we associate. As I stated, it would be ideal to try to establish love in the family, but also emphasize that love for all of God's children is desirable. Along with love, the family unit provides opportunities to learn many other socially beneficial characteristics. Let us talk about some of the many things that can be learned from the dynamics of the family structure.

Family is the first place that we are exposed to the reality that there is a hierarchy in many relationships. This applies to school, work, the military or some sort of grass roots community organization. There has to be levels of command with someone being in charge. There should also be descending levels of command and corresponding decreased levels of authority. The family is where we learn that mom and dad run the household, and with good reason. They are the oldest, have the most life experience, the most education, the most money and they are paying the bills. They have been through the most and can tell you from their own personal experiences or the experiences of their peers what choices are the wisest in various situations.

Another lesson that can be learned in the family is the understanding of sharing. If you have two parents and three siblings in the household, but only two restrooms, it is obvious that all five members of the residence are unable to use the bathrooms simultaneously. This being the case, you must learn use the restroom to relieve yourself along with taking care of any other hygienic concerns, being mindful that you are not the only home occupant and others need access to the restroom as well. Sharing is also learned when it comes to dining. Regardless of how deliciously the meal has been prepared, you can't strive to eat everything available. First of all, you would become miserable from consuming too much. Secondly, such a selfish approach would deny other family members the needed nutrition that they require to be healthy.

Family is the first place where we develop a sense of responsibility. The fact that our parents require us to make our own beds, vacuum our own rooms, hang up our clothes and place dirty clothes in the laundry hamper gives us our initial jobs. It is not uncommon for us to have to cut the grass or assist in raking up leaves. Our parents are not being difficult in requiring us to do these activities. They simply have the awareness to understand that we must become accustomed to doing work. They are preparing us to have the discipline necessary to succeed in school and life, so their requirements are actually gestures of love.

It is in the family where we are taught a sense of respect for authority. If we do not do what our parents ask of us, there are repercussions. This will happen to us later in our lives as well, so we should all consider ourselves blessed to have had parents who were caring enough to raise us in such a way that we knew that certain behavioral expectations must be met, or there would be less than pleasant outcomes. This prepares us for proper and reasonable behavior in life.

Lastly, the family is where we learn that we are going to be held accountable for our actions. We live in a society that tells us "ignorance of the law is no excuse." That means that even if you do not know the law, you will not be given a free pass. That's a tough lesson to learn in your twenties or thirties. Families that hold their children accountable instill in their descendants that you cannot do anything you want to do. You cannot impose your will on others or take what does not belong to you. You can't damage property belonging to others and expect to get away with it.

It simply does not work that way. I see so many selfish, self-centered people in this society. I wonder how many come from a family where their parents did not instill in them some of the basic characteristics that we have just discussed. I truly believe we can build a better global family if each of us does our best to structure our immediate family in such a way that sharing, responsibility, love, respect for authority and accountability are emphasized.

Community

Webster's New World Dictionary defines community as follows: any group living in the same area or having interest, work, etc. in common. This means, in my interpretation, that you can have artist community, the Latin community, the Black community, the business community, etc. We have spoken previously about two of the four things that I have stated that I think are the most important things we can focus upon (love and family). I want to share now how we can link those two with a focus on community.

We talked about the importance of love being unconditional. We discussed how love is about creating a place of emotional refuge. We spoke about how love could be that buffer that prompts you to find the motivation to diffuse heated exchanges to the extent that the exchanges do not elevate into physical confrontation.

We talked about family. We addressed the different lessons that can be extracted from proper family interactions, things like having a hierarchy in any group, the importance of sharing, the need to have duties, a sense of responsibility and the importance of accountability. If each of us focuses on our particular family unit on our respective block, I think we can say with confidence that that block will be full of the right type of energy, the type of block that people feel comfortable residing in and returning to after a day at school or work. I think we will be able to say with confidence that because of the type of love and family dynamics that were emphasized collectively on these blocks, there will be a higher likelihood that the people who come from these areas will be more inclined to be productive citizens who have a greater potential to do good in the world. Now, if we can expand this practice from a block to a subdivision, we are talking about an even larger number of people who have the correct thoughts and ways of interaction that lead to a better way of life. So what I am getting at is this. No one person has to change the world by themselves. If each of us focuses on our family and our particular neighborhood, then imagine the impact that that may have on our respective communities and ultimately the world. How might this all occur? Here is an example.

Since nothing happens in a vacuum, people from other parts of the city who interact with residents of that block or subdivision driven by love and proper family structure will have no option other than to feel the good that radiates from that healthy area of town with which they have just intermingled. They may become elevated by the love and correct family structure that they experience. If they are adults and have a family, perhaps they will be inspired to incorporate some of the tendencies that they have witnessed. People of a youthful nature (children) who come from a different part of the city but have a chance to witness the discipline of their peers may also recognize a corresponding tendency of their peers from the well-structured families and neighborhoods to be well behaved and high performing in school. Since people closest to us tend to influence us the most, this increases the likelihood that the children from the other neighborhoods may observe the tendencies of their peers that lead to better academic performance- listening well, taking good notes, studying daily and not cramming for examinations at the last minute- and be prompted to mirror some of these same habits. So the point I strive to make is that we should not drive ourselves crazy trying to change the world. Maybe if we do good right where we are, the impact will be meaningful. Truly this makes sense when we consider, again, that nothing happens in a vacuum and all that we do has an impact on something or someone. Remember, each family and each community is simply a microcosm of the global family or the global community. If each of us focuses on our respective families and our respective communities in terms of attempting to bring about a state of health, the world can't help but be impacted in a positive way.

But I do not want to stop there. Aside from affecting our communities by the fact that nothing happens in a vacuum and all the good that we do naturally touches others, I would like to suggest some active things we can do that are specific to the Black community.

If we stop for a second and write down a few of the concerns that we have in our community as people of African descent, we will be better prepared to have certain issues to target as points of correction. Bullying for one is a national concern now. However, people in the know can tell you that bullying has been an issue in the Black community for a long time. Certainly I do not suggest this is the result of some sort of genetic predisposition on the behalf of people of color. Yet when you consider all the issues confronting Blacks disproportionately (single parent homes, economic instability, limited male role models, absence of Black History, etc.) that have created in many of us a sense of powerlessness, we should not be surprised when we observe unnecessary physical force being used by some of our children. These feelings of powerlessness coupled with perpetual anger on the behalf of many of our children are a recipe for bullying. So, let us start dealing with the issue of bullying by looking at the root causes of this type of behavior, and start addressing those core concerns. Additionally, let us consider the benefits of making self-defense classes more readily available to victims of bullying so that they may be better prepared to defend themselves against their attackers when necessary. Also, let us try to be mindful of where our children are at all times. We should strive to make sure they are never alone. There are predators in our midst. Typically they look for an easy target. That target is less desirable when adults are around visibly as our children transition from one location to another. Moreover, some of us adults want to make an impact on our community but do not know how. Let us consider becoming a member of Big Brother Big Sister of America. This is a national organization, with chapters all over. By joining such an organization, we position ourselves to be role models and help fill the void often caused by single parent homes. Furthermore, the more our youth interact with people of African descent that are productive and driven by concern, the more likely that our children will be well adjusted and more inclined to be successful in how they deal with others and possibly how they perform in school. Finally, let us consider creating Rites of Passage programs in our communities. These were common in Africa. Some exist here in the United States, and there have been reports of how beneficial these programs have been on the development of our children.

These are just a few ideas that we can consider acting upon. This is not an exhaustive list, just ideas to get the ball rolling.

Purpose

What is purpose? I think "purpose" and "destiny" are one and the same. I think both these words suggest that we all have been manifested into flesh for a reason. The tricky part is that I do not know if any of us is given a written document at birth telling us what it is that we are supposed to do while our souls inhabit this physical shell. Typically we find out what our purpose is or figure it out with the assistance of extensive spiritual study. Other times, life prompts you to conclude that you must make certain decisions, or changes, if you want to find peace. This is an example, I think, of the universe intervening and forcing you to change your lifestyle until that lifestyle is consistent with the reason you have been brought here. I can tell you from my own life that strange things have happened to me throughout my existence. I have no doubt at all that the universe has been active in moving my life in a certain direction. I would like to take this time to share some of these experiences with you now if you don't mind.

Growing up as a young boy on the North side of Richmond, Va., it became apparent to me very early that I could outrun nearly all my peers. It was effortless for me. I even had friends who would ask, "Man, where did you get that speed from." I participated briefly with a local track club in Richmond that was known as the "Virginia Comets." I left shortly afterwards for some childish reason on my behalf. However, my speed was so exceptional that one of the track coaches for months and maybe a few years afterward would ask my father about me, telling him time and again that he had never seen a little boy run so fast. I must have been eight or nine years old at the time, but I remember it like it was yesterday.

Fast forward a few years and I am playing little league football in the sixth grade. The name of the squad was the Laurel Panthers. Again, my speed was evident, as I was the fastest player on my team. I was on the midget junior varsity. On occasion we would scrimmage the midget varsity. I was faster than anyone there also. One person was my equal. His name was Eric Cooper. Other than that, out of about 40 young boys, only one could match my foot speed. All that changed in a year's time.

My seventh-grade year, I again played for the Panthers. This time I played with what we called the "juniors." I observed something very odd early into the practices. Some of the same guys that I could outrun the previous year were now blowing by me. Brian Bailey was one that came to mind. Initially I thought well maybe Brian had gotten that much faster, and he had, but when we were timed for the 50-yard dash in gym class, my time was .6 slower than it was the year before. Somehow I had slowed down even though I was a year older and theoretically a year physically more mature. Even as a twelve-year-old this logically made no sense to me. Then I noticed my friend who lived in the same cul-de-sac with me began to close the gap on me as well until he too could run as fast as me. Again, to me this made no logical sense. Since my neighbor was my best friend and my play partner, whatever activities he was doing (foot races, dodge ball, basketball, football) were activities I participated in as well since we were inseparable at the time. That being the case, the same physical activities that inspired his physical improvement should have affected me in the same way, but it didn't. For years, I tried to make sense of this, but was unable to do so. This trend of my peers evolving physically but me stagnating continued all the way until my junior year in high school. At this point, I had become determined to do what was necessary to recapture that feeling of freedom and power that my youthful speed had once granted me. I began running sprints on my own. I also began jogging and doing other calisthenics. By the time I was seventeen, the explosiveness had started to return, but by that time I had grown disenchanted with school and was unable to keep my grades high enough to be on a sports team. So while I had contemplated running track my senior year, my lack of academic focus negated that option.

Years came and went. I continued to work out because it helped me deal with my feelings of alienation and not fitting in. However, something else odd would occur to me whenever I would attempt to play basketball. I would get injured every time. Once I got elbowed in the eye and the mouth simultaneously, chipping one of my teeth. Another time, while in graduate school, a full back sized individual got fooled by one of my pump fakes on the basketball court and fell on me. Years later, there was a separate incident where I sustained an injury on the court, somehow without even being touched. This incident was particularly strange because after the last game that day, I walked off the court feeling no discomfort anywhere. However, I wake up the next morning and my body is making an audible cracking sound with each step. I am thinking, "What in the world is this?" No one ran into me. I had not fallen down. I walked off the court with no pain and no need for assistance. What was going on? Finally, a few more years went by and I was playing basketball again. Mind you that I played infrequently, maybe a couple of times per year at the most. My basketball playing after the age of twenty was mostly confined to games of "h-o-r-s-e" or shooting contests, so the odds of me obtaining injury were minor since I did not engage actively in games often enough to have a high probability of sustaining injury. Anyway, years later, I somehow pulled a shoulder muscle in a game playing basketball. My shoulder took about two years to heal. At this point, I decided to never play in a game of basketball again. I think I was 31 years old at the time, and I have not played a game since then. I have just continued to shoot around and work on solo moves and ball handling drills, but no games.

The funny thing about this basketball experience of mine is that I stayed in shape, always lifting weights, running, performing calisthenics, etc., so it is not like I was injured because my body was not prepared for physical activity. Additionally, I have witnessed other people who play basketball every weekend for years with no mouthpiece and no jock strap and go injury free. Again this made no logical sense to me. It seemed to me that anyone that played that frequently would increase the likelihood of injury simply because they did it so often. Then it dawned on me: Throughout my life, my physical gifts had either mysteriously eroded, or if through my sheer determination I was able to regain those gifts, injuries would occur. At some point I began to believe that more than bad luck was involved. At some point I concluded that someone (The Most High?) did not want me to place so much of my attention on my physical self or my physical development. It was as if circumstances were conspiring to move me away from dwelling on physical expressions like athletics. I began to conclude that the universe had other plans for me, and that is why I have had the experiences that I have had. It was at this point that I decided to concentrate on other aspects of my being (the mental and the spiritual) to see if I could make sense of it all and hopefully meet with less resistance.

This is one example of what I meant earlier when I was suggesting that maybe the universe at times keeps you from moving in certain directions in life because that direction is not consistent with your destiny. Looking back on it, it all makes sense now.

I think that the universe also brings people, opportunities, and circumstances into your life to further your progress toward living your purpose, even when you are not aware of it at the time. For example, after High School, I enrolled at a local Community College and specialized in Liberal Arts. I was not sure what I wanted to do with my life and felt that majoring in Liberal Arts would give me the comprehensive exposure to a wide range of different topics, thus giving me a better chance to find out what might interest me. A light bulb went off when I took my first Psychology course. The study of the human mind, how it processes information, and the study of how we think and respond to certain experiences was particularly stimulating for me. I subsequently decided to transfer to V.C.U. (Virginia Commonwealth University) and majored in Psychology. Majoring in Psychology allowed me to additionally study Sociology and Logic. What's the significance of this, you may ask? Well, I have been a rapper since the age of 15. By studying Sociology, I have become a much better conscious emcee (another name for a rapper) because of my understanding of social dynamics and how they shape one's decisions and life. As I stated previously, studying Psychology gives me a better understanding of how people think. This awareness from both these disciplines positions me better to "drop science" (be instructive) in a song that I would lack otherwise. I had no idea what I would do after High School. I never knew I would major in Psychology, but I believe the universe did those things necessary to prompt me to study the Humanities. Lastly, anyone who majors in one of the Humanities (English, Psychology, Social Work, History, etc.) is required to read extensively and to write a great deal. Both of these requirements have prepared me to feel comfortable speaking on live television about issues relevant to people of color. These experiences have also lessened my apprehensiveness about writing and fleshing out my thoughts.

What happened when I began doing the things that I thought I had been called to do (conscious rap, performing my music on stages, presentations on live television and radio, being part of community driven organizations, etc.)? I noticed myself finding my job stress to be a less dominant factor in my life. I began to realize more and more that there is more to life than working a 9-5 for forty years, becoming old and arthritic and dying. I began to see how I could do good deeds with the understanding I had amassed from years of reading coupled with my educational background. As I began to do more and more in terms of community driven activities, I began to look forward to rising in the morning. Life started becoming less of a burden and more of an opportunity to fulfill what I was starting to believe to be my purpose. This excitement has given me the ability to mentally minimize the madness that often occurs on the job. I find myself realizing that a job is just a source of income. Jobs do not define me. I had been counting my blessings for years, but when your life conditions do not change with time, one can feel like merely counting your blessings is self-delusion. However, counting one's blessings coupled with finding your purpose and being active in that or those activities brings about a peace that counting blessings alone doesn't provide. What does that mean? It means that if we want to find peace we should strive to find our purpose or destiny. Our lack of awareness of it could very well be the source of our discontent. It may also be the reason why many of us fail at certain endeavors even when we try mightily to be successful. Again, I believe the universe will block "the way" if that activity is not consistent with your destiny. However, it seems when we have been successful in identifying our purpose and began actively indulging in it, the obstacles seem to vanish.

Now this is where it gets good. If we can all agree that we all have a purpose, a reason for being, then it is logical to deduce that none of our lives is purely accidental. And if we can look at all human beings as having a reason for being, we should be better able to respect one another if only because we recognize the universe has a purpose in mind for everyone.

It is said that divinity is in all humans. What if we are all simply soldiers for the Most High who have been manifested into flesh to do the work of God in the physical realm? What if each of us took the time to specifically attempt to identify what God would do if he were here? What if we found out that one of the things that God would want us to achieve is the ability to love regardless of outward appearances? What if God wants us to assist one another so that we can all have the necessities of life? What if we subsequently concluded that if God were here, he would endeavor to help us evolve spiritually to develop a oneness with him? I think most people who have pursued their destiny will tell you that the more that they serve others, the more obstacles seem to vanish from their lives. This suggests to me that serving is possibly a part of why we have come into being in the physical form. Maybe we have all come to help one another reach a higher plane, and being active in showing love, embracing family, community and purpose all work together to achieve that end.

Let Us Be Proactive

I remember back when I was in graduate school, a classmate and I were talking casually. I was growing daily in terms of my political awareness and was beginning to dress in a way that was consistent with that consciousness. I mentioned to her that I wanted to acquire a dashiki, a traditional West African shirt. She laughed without malice, saying something to the effect that I wanted to bring back the 70s. And while I was not offended by her comment because I knew there was no harmful intent in her words, I did find myself feeling awkward. I felt awkward because in my mind I did not want the dashiki to be merely confined to the decade of the 70s as something that should be found in a time capsule. I saw the wearing of a dashiki as a means to acknowledge my African roots. For me, acknowledging who I am is a lifestyle, something that I intend to do until I transition. It is not something that I do for one day or even a decade and discard. Far too often, we as black folks reduce traditional garb and cultural practices to mere fads, thus confining them to the status of temporary things of interest. It is time for us to realize that some things should be a way of life.

I remember when the Rodney King beating by Los Angeles police took place. After the not guilty verdict was announced, Black folks took to the streets and began protesting in a way that they felt would finally get the attention of those in power: They began burning everything in sight and looting buildings. The news channels showed footage of enraged Blacks carrying banners that read "No Justice No Peace." Shortly thereafter, a gang truce was announced between the Crips and The Bloods. While I am thrilled at the fact that Black folks were starting to demonstrate some understanding of the power of unity as evidenced by the "No Justice No Peace" banners and the truce among gangs, I was forced to ask the question, "Why must there be a tragedy before we as a people began coming together to work towards common goals?" I noticed the same type of response in recent times to the deaths of Trayvon Martin, Sandra Bland, Freddy Gray, Eric Garner and Philando Castile. Again, I ask why must we wait for a tragedy to motivate us to be community driven when that should be a daily focus.

After all, we do not brush our teeth only when we have a cavity. We brush them daily, often at least twice a day for basic oral hygiene and maintenance of that hygiene. We floss nightly. We do not wait until the dentist informs us that gum disease has settled in. We shower or bathe daily. We do not wait until we become malodorous or become infected with germs or a disease associated with a lack of body cleansing. We do all these things proactively to prevent problems and to maintain whatever current state of health we presently possess. Should we not be as proactive in ensuring that the health of our communities is maintained? Certainly we should do this. We just have probably never been prompted to look at community health this way. Well, today is a new day, and I think it is time we start putting things in place to make sure our communities remain healthy, much in the same way that we are diligent in keeping our bodies healthy.

What are some of the things that we can do to maintain community health? I have made some suggestions previously, particularly in the prior essay "What is Black." I also made some suggestions in the essay "Love, Family, Community and Purpose" about things we can embrace as continual practices to create and maintain community health. Here is a list of the activities:

1. Create Community Monitoring Groups
2. Establish Study Groups
3. Create and/or support Holistically Structured Schools
4. Take trips to locations on the planet that showcase the ingenuity of African people
5. Address bullying (help the bullies develop a means of saying "I Am." Make the martial arts accessible to the victims of bullying)
6. Turn our communities into villages
7. Become a mentor to youth
8. Create and maintain Rites of Passage Programs
9. Invite African entrepreneurs to speak about how to start businesses

Yes, it is time to become active in maintaining a healthy community. In the same way that brushing daily and flossing daily minimizes the tartar buildup on our teeth and make the dental visit less traumatic, incorporating some of the above suggestions along with other ideas just may help us create healthier living areas.

Love for Serena Williams

When Serena Williams won her twenty second grand slam title, there was a great deal of venom directed at her on social media. I found the hatred to be horrendous and totally unjustifiable. How could anyone bring themselves to say some of the ugly things that they did about Serena? Shouldn't we be proud as Americans that she had tied the great Steffi Graf? Shouldn't we be proud that Serena has opened the door to the possibility - mentally, at least- that other young, African females can succeed in the world of tennis? Why not embrace someone who has demonstrated discipline, persistence and hard work to achieve what had previously appeared unreachable by so many people of African descent. As far as I know, Serena has not done anything to prompt the general population to treat her so badly. She has never been arrested for committing a crime. She has not been charged with public drunkenness or been observed urinating on public facilities. There have been no recorded brawls in which she was a participant. She has not been arrested for drug use or distribution. So again, I ask why is there so much malice shown towards her?

It is documented that Serena has financed the construction of two schools in Kenya. It has been said that Serena requires that at least 40% of the students be female. Apparently, Serena is aware that sexism can be universal and undereducated females are less prepared to do for themselves, thus making them more vulnerable to exploitation. In 2015, two males from the schools that Serena financed were accepted to college. This level of academic success is unprecedented in the region where the Williams' financed schools exist. Furthermore, as of January 2016, Serena had financed four years of college for six young people and was paying the bills of dozens more (S.L. Price, 2016). Does this sound like the monster that so many on social media have made her out to be?

Some claim that they love America, but hate the greatest AMERICAN female tennis player (and probably the greatest period) who has lived thus far. We talk about "lifting yourself up by the bootstraps," but are unwilling to acknowledge that Serena comes from Compton, was not born into privilege, had no large number of prior African descended female players from which to derive inspiration, did not have a neighborhood of young African descended females to play tennis with growing up, and was probably told directly and indirectly that she could only do so much in a "white" sport.

She has been said to look manly (I vehemently disagree). Some have suggested that she is on steroids even though her physique was obviously muscular even as a teenager. Additionally, the argument for steroid consumption is annihilated when we consider that Serena is randomly tested year-round and has NEVER come up positive. She has always been a top player, not one who made an unbelievable jump in performance that defies explanation, a typical red flag for steroid users (e.g., Ben Johnson). Finally, an objective viewing of Serena performing confirms that with all her formidable physical gifts (power, quickness, stamina and flexibility), her greatest attributes may be her mental toughness, tennis IQ and her ability to play in more than one style. And if this is not enough, she has learned to speak French and was attending some aspect of fashion design school at one time to expand her means of generating an income and use all her talents, physical and artistic, to maximize her human potential.

I am here to tell you, ladies and gentlemen, Serena Williams is not just a great tennis player. The fact that she has beaten ALL the odds confirms that SHE is the American dream.

Long live the Queen!

Responding to Hate

Regardless of what it is that you do, you will encounter haters. I don't care if you are a promoter of shows, a song producer, studio engineer, comedian, architect, dancer, slam poet, rapper, singer, song writer, entrepreneur, painter, chess player, etc. You will always have those who gravitate towards the negative and feel the need to try to minimize what you do, often when they can't do it as well as you. But that's not the point, so let me not digress. The point is to emphasize that hate is inevitable. The question we must ask ourselves is, "How am I going to respond to this dark energy?" Well, we can respond in a few different ways. We could get angry with the person that approaches us with the venom. We could get into a verbal or a physical confrontation with that individual. We could go home and tear some things up, but I don't think these would be particularly positive ways to respond. We may become emotionally wounded, sink into a funk and discontinue trying. Again, I don't think these responses are ideal either. Let me suggest a more productive way to deal with other peoples' negative interactions with us.

When people disrespect you, why not smile at the dim witted, self-loathing individual and give them no more energy than that. Instead, shortly thereafter document what that person said along with the date and time the hate was verbalized. Keep this recorded incident accessible. Maybe you want to keep it in your cell phone. Perhaps you prefer to maintain the incident on an index card that you keep taped to your refrigerator. Either way, each time someone comes out of their mouth wrong, add that additional insult. Now, whenever you find yourself lacking motivation to refine your craft, refer to the slights people hurled your way. Read the statements you've recorded verbatim, and feel the rage surging in your body. However, instead of wasting that energy doing something destructive, channel that energy to inspire you to work smarter and more efficiently towards becoming better at what you do (refer to the previous essay "How to Avoid Unnecessary Competition"). If you use this strategy of focusing your energy intelligently, you can't help but become better at your craft. And as you continue to grow, it will become more and more evident to those who experience your talents that you are slowly becoming more than just a talented person in your field. At some point, they will be compelled to recognize that you are becoming a FORCE OF NATURE.

Some may ask, "But why shouldn't I curse the hater out? Am I not letting them off the hook by not letting them feel my fury?" I would say not really. Let us consider that negative people manifest who they are inside with the words that they speak. In other words, haters are often despicable people who come from environments where negativity rules. Darkness and hate are zones of familiarity for them, so to engage them in that way only takes them back to the place where they most frequently reside emotionally. Why do them that favor? Also, we all have heard the saying that "misery loves company." Some people, as sad as it may sound, derive feelings of contentment from making others feel badly because they are unhappy. Why give them the satisfaction that they desire? Finally, let us remember that the thing that a hater wants most is for you to meet with a lack of success. They feed off those thoughts. They celebrate when others fail. So, with that in mind, we need to be cognizant that the best revenge against our detractors is our success. That will hurt them in the long run much more than a verbal tongue lashing. Yes, you can curse them out, but if you give up because of what they have said, they have won. We must fight, yes, but our combat strategy should be an intelligent one.

Uncle Larry's Views

(I have always stated that the two most intelligent men that I have encountered in my life were my father, Prince Earl Reid, Sr., and my Uncle Larry (dad's brother). Neither one of these gentlemen ever attended college, but they both possess a depth of thought, perception and ability to think abstractly that exceeds many of the professionally educated persons that I know. It is only natural, therefore, that I have been blessed to document and share with you the thoughts of at least one of these gentlemen. In this case, I speak of my Uncle Larry. What follows is a synopsis of a question and answer session Uncle Larry and I had where I played the role of the interviewer. But first, before we get into the question and answer section, Uncle Larry provided an introductory series of statements that I have summarized and provided for your consumption. Here, now, are Uncle Larry's openings statements. The question and answer section immediately follow.)

Uncle Larry started by mentioning that we (African people) have lost the "hookup," that unifying force that brings people together. What is this "hookup" that my Uncle speaks of? He went on to further speak about an "entity" that unifies people. He then clarified that the "entity" to which he was referring was religion. I found this to be interesting. "Religion" has been defined by Ra UN Nefer Amen as that thing that reconnects or links us back to God, deities or the spirit realm (Amen, 1990). How appropriate, I thought, that Uncle Larry had used the term "hookup" when referring to religion. Apparently, he understood instinctively that religion or spirituality can connect us with something bigger than us, but let us continue.

My Uncle spoke about specific Bible incidents, particularly the enslavement of the Tribes of Israel and the ultimate exodus of the Jewish people. What he found interesting is that when the Jews initially entered Kemet (renamed Egypt), they came as twelve different tribes. However, the collective oppression forced a bonding of the tribes so that when they left they were no longer twelve individual tribes. Their collective hardships had prompted a unity amongst the former twelve tribes. Upon the freeing of the Jews, they now perceived of themselves as The Nation of Israel. What "entity" was it that unified the people? According to the Bible and Uncle Larry's interpretation, it was religion. He mentioned that the people of Israel now had one religion and one God. He seems to think that these two factors further minimized separatism into tribes, which served to solidify and strengthen the Jewish people. He also spoke of the Mosaic Law and how these documented laws of conduct would serve to shape the conduct of the Jewish people, and specify that certain behavior was not acceptable.

Whether or not you believe or accept the Torah is not the question here. I think the thing we should extract from what my Uncle has stated is the power of unity, and the importance of finding something under which to unify. I believe Uncle Larry was trying to get us to understand that this same undeniable unity demonstrated by Jews has been a major contributor to the present global economic and political strength demonstrated by the Jews up to this present day.

Now, allow me to digress. I am fully aware that the original Jews were of African descent (Pimienta-Bey, 2002). However, the same thing applies. The same unity of the original Jews, also called Moors, led to the ability of the Jews/Moors to collectively elevate the artistic, medical, architectural and cultural existence of Spain upon their arrival in the 8th century. That is the point, the power of unity.

Remember, as my Uncle has clarified, Europeans once openly acknowledged their ethnic differences, referring once to themselves as Russian, German, Italian, French, Spanish, etc. In fact, America formerly discriminated against both the Irish and Italian immigrants in this country (Bennett, 1982). Now, as my Uncle clarified, when you apply for a job and are requested on the application to specify your ethnicity, the categories have become literally a lot more Black and White. The application does not ask if you are Russian, Polish, Italian, Welsh, etc. It asks are you White, Black (of non-Latin descent), Asian or Latin. Europeans have come to understand the power of unity, it seems.

Uncle Larry further indicated that he had observed that many of the principles of The Constitution are derived from Biblical moral codes. He seemed to want to demonstrate that the American Nation (as we presently know it) was founded upon the unifying power of religion. Again we see, in the eyes of my Uncle, how religion has helped to unify a people and been instrumental in shaping the direction of a country. What I took from my Uncle's opening statement is that we as African people should attempt to use religion or spirituality to do more than help us "catch the spirit" on Sunday. He confirmed this by saying "that it is not about the bounce," meaning that it is okay to be moved emotionally, but we should strive to find a practical application of Religion. My belief is that my

Uncle thinks that we can use it to help us unify, enhance our communities, build our own nation, minimize our own tribalism and create laws and codes of conduct that are acceptable and beneficial to the masses of Africans.

What We Should Be Focused Upon

I next began the process of asking Uncle Larry different questions, the first of which is, "What do you think that we as a people should be focused upon?" He answered that when we look out we must ask ourselves "are we happy with where we are?" So it seems that he thinks that one of the first things that we should do is to observe the conditions of the Black community and try to identify if there are specific concerns that we need to address. We can start by looking at the five main components that impact the quality of our lives. Those five areas are economics, education, politics, culture and spirituality. We can go further and deeper and identify more specific issues and behaviors that apply particularly to the five aforementioned areas. This analysis of the condition of African people is necessary prior to us attempting to make any corrections. After all, if we have not first accurately pinpointed specific things that require improvement, we can fall victim to speaking to non-factors- improving on things that don't really need our focus. In addition to us looking out to identify areas for improvement, Uncle Larry said we should next ask ourselves if "I can contribute something to this?" This suggests that we must do some self-assessment and identify what talents, skills and abilities each of us possesses as individuals, and then ask ourselves how we can use whatever talents we have to speak to some of the problems that plague our people. One of our impediments, though, is that we have been "deceived by our own people." This can prompt us to support people who look like us physically but do not possess the needed concern for the Black community to benefit us. An example of our being deceived and our blind allegiance, says my Uncle, is our willingness to vote someone into political office simply based upon the color of their skin. In my Uncle's opinion, "it is not good at all to not have questions." As the rap group Public Enemy once stated, "Every brother aint a brother, 'cause a Black hand squeezed on Malcolm X the man." He seems to suggest that we need to be mindful of this and question every one regardless of ethnicity. Only by questioning will we allow ourselves to do the necessary investigating to determine if someone deserves our allegiance. Finally, Uncle Larry, being cognizant that we can always use some assistance, suggests that we should "seek positive people to make this happen" (address the problem areas that plague our communities by finding those with the necessary skills, experience and concern). He thinks that this is where our attention should be directed.

Black Lives Matter

I thought it would be interesting to get Uncle Larry's thoughts on the "Black Lives Matter" movement. It is such a news garnering organization at present that I thought it would be ideal to discuss. "You don't know how this shoe fits until you put this shoe on," says my Uncle, paraphrasing the ageless adage that speaks to putting yourself in someone else's shoes to have a better understanding of their discomfort. Uncle Larry mentioned the fact that no one has ever said White lives DON'T matter, but there are some who are opposed to any movement that unifies people that are classified as African

American. My Uncle was quick to additionally add that "all lives matter." He made sure to acknowledge that. The problem as he sees it is that it is obvious that white lives matter when we look at the treatment this society has afforded people of European descent. The same treatment often eludes us. For instance, he spoke of how Pat Robertson and his Christian Broadcasting Network (CBN) have provided support to the Nation of Israel and the global Jewish community by unapologetically highlighting efforts to assist those of the Jewish faith. No one is "jumping on Pat" (Robertson) for providing coverage of Jewish concerns. People seem willing to acknowledge their difficult past and freely accept missions to aid. It is only when we (African people) start unifying, begin consciously working toward our own improvement or enlightenment, or start seeking financial assistance is there some sort of backlash. But let us use specific examples to make this more evident for those still skeptical of the inconsistencies.

No one seems to blink when a Jewish museum is constructed to acknowledge the Jewish Holocaust. However, as soon as the African American Museum in D.C. was erected this past month (September 2016), there was an immediate negative response to it by some of my brethren of European descent. When Sandra Bland ended up dead resulting from some routine police stop and questioning, the outcry from Whites was relatively minor. Even white females were relatively quiet. But can you imagine the ridiculous amount of outrage that would have been shown if Sandra Bland were White and the officer on duty was of African descent. If that woman had shown no more physical resistance than the real Sandra Bland had shown and still came up dead, there would have been rage like you could not imagine. However, centuries of enslavement, rape, castration, lynching, land theft, segregation and false propaganda against African people have desensitized society to our mistreatment. People have seemingly lost their ability to feel anything when we are harmed. It is almost as if we have been kicked and beat down for so long that it is now accepted conduct. But let's give a few more examples.

What if Trayvon Martin was a 140-pound teenager who just happened to be White? What if he was returning from the store after purchasing some Skittles and a can of iced tea and was headed to his father's place of residence? What if he had not been observed committing any crime? He had not been seen attempting to enter anyone's residence by force, nor had he been seen breaking into anyone's automobile. He was simply your normal White teen with a hoody on (it was raining) strolling casually through the community. What if a 250-pound grown Black man had called 911 and informed them of the White teen with the hoody, and 911 had informed the grown Black man to sit back and allow the police to investigate? What if that 250-pound Black man disregarded the directions of 911 and proceeded to approach the young teen? Some altercation ensued with the result being that the teen ended up being murdered. Would Whites have been as accepting as they were with the murder of the real Trayvon if the ethnicities were in reverse? I have to say that I doubt it. In fact, there has been documentation that George Zimmerman (Trayvon's murderer) received hundreds of thousands of dollars in financial support for his pending trial. Think about it. You murder a Black boy who commits no crime and you receive massive amounts of monetary help. What does that say about the value of a Black life?

Finally, let us speak about Freddy Gray, the young man who died in police custody in Baltimore in April 2015. It has been said that Freddy had been restrained by officers with his hands handcuffed behind his back. The story further goes that Freddy was overheard asking for his inhaler because he was having difficulty breathing. No inhaler was provided. Additionally, when Mr. Gray was placed in the police van to transport him, he was not restrained properly which led to his body being bounced around violently as the van traveled to the station. It has been stated that Mr. Gray was heard asking for help in the van. An additional passenger had been picked up and was the individual that confirmed hearing Freddy Gray's complaints of discomfort and statements indicating he could not breathe. These complaints went disregarded. Whether or not Mr. Gray had committed a crime is not the question, nor is it the issue. The issue is that he had been handcuffed and posed no threat to anyone because of this, yet his very basic needs went unaddressed and he ended up dying from complications of a spinal cord that was "80% severed." If his life mattered, would he have been treated so callously? It is these precise moments of indifference that prompts us to say, "Black Lives Matter." We must make it known that we are human and deserve to be treated with the same concern that other ethnic groups receive automatically. We didn't create the need to say, "Black Lives Matter." The need was made evident by the disregard for our lives that is as common as a bird flying on the winds or a dog barking at a passerby.

Uncle Larry says he is "very proud of a young man that has protested" the recent and historical incidents of disregard shown towards African people, obviously referring to Colin Kaepernick. He stated that he was proud that Colin had the courage to stand up (or not stand, actually) to protest what he perceives to be continual injustice even in the face of the opposition that he would inevitably face- being told to "go to Canada" or wherever.

"Racism has never been truly addressed in America," says my Uncle. A lack of equality continues to be an issue that we as African people confront. Some seem oblivious to this obvious truth. Colin Kaepernick, in Uncle Larry's view, has decided that until equality is a reality for all, he will take his stand by taking a knee.

"Black Lives Matter."

Land of the Free?

Earlier in this year's pro football season, the San Francisco 49er's backup Quarterback (Colin Kaepernick) decided to kneel during the ceremonial playing of the National Anthem prior to the game as opposed to standing. Furthermore, he was observed being seen not placing his right hand over his heart during the playing of the Anthem. When asked about his behavior during the playing of the Anthem, Mr. Kaepernick said that events in recent years regarding excessive police force and historical mistreatment of people of African descent prompted him to feel the need to show that he was opposed to our treatment, and he was not interested in just accepting what he perceived to be continual injustice without him voicing his discontent in some way. What started as a silent, singular example of protest has become an event that speaks to questions concerning Race, excessive police force, historical racism, intolerance, indifference, guilt and defensiveness. I want to talk about the variety of issues that Colin Kaepernick's protest has brought to the surface. Hopefully, this opportunity to address certain tendencies in this country will give us all an opportunity to elevate our ability to be a "kinder, gentler" nation, in the words of George H. W. Bush.

In response to Mr. Kaepernick's actions regarding the National Anthem, we found many people burning replicas of his football jersey. Other people have been seen placing doormats at the entrance of their businesses or homes that contained Mr. Kaepernick's jersey number and team colors. Mike Ditka, NFL (National Football League) hall of fame tight end and former coach of the Super Bowl winning Chicago Bears, said in response to Kaepernick's actions that he loves his country and his flag too, and if Kaepernick was unhappy he should leave the country.

Wait a minute. Just because you publicly disagree with the social policies of your country does not mean that you hate your homeland. Mike Ditka in saying that he "loves his country and his flag too" and seemingly using that as an excuse to disregard the historical racism and mistreatment that has fueled Kaepernick's protest is analogous to allowing a family member or a child to run rampant, imposing their will on others and causing immeasurable harm just because you feel affectionately towards them. This does the family member no good. If their behavior goes unchecked, they will continue to navigate through this life and interact with others in a continuously harmful way. They have never been questioned for their actions or been held accountable for the pain they may have caused, so why would they consider changing. This ultimately stunts the social development of the family member, possibly setting them up to be seen as malicious, selfish and incorrigible. If we are to continue to speak analogously, then we must say that Kaepernick's actions are more consistent with a loving family member or parent that corrects the other with the hope of trying to help them grow to be more concerned and more aware of the impact of their actions on others. Additionally, the world is watching. We do not want America to be perceived as a country that allows for the mistreatment of some of her citizens, do we? We have always been told that America is the great "melting pot." If that is truly the case, all ethnicities must be allowed to benefit from this "stew" of freedoms and opportunities equally. Colin Kaepernick is showing love to his ethnic group and America by reminding her to live up to her great potential and her wonderful ideals that are laid out in her Constitution. This is an example of love: helping someone, or your country, be the best that they can be.

I was surprised and disappointed by the responses of my fellow Americans and Mike Ditka. I personally saw nothing wrong with Kaepernick's stance. He did not burn the flag. He did not initiate any physical confrontation with anyone in general or anyone on the police force. He did not shoot at or murder any police officers. His protest was silent and respectful, but necessary, in my opinion. But let's continue this discussion.

Protest is as American as apple pie. Who remembers the "Boston Tea Party," that incident in the New England area a few centuries back where Samuel Adams and The Sons of Liberty threw 342 chests of tea overboard to protest what they referred to as "taxation without representation." Every American youth has been informed about this incident at some point in their educational process. This incident has been presented as a significant moment in American history, one that should bring us pride, but let's not stop there. Patrick Henry has been praised for centuries for his famous "give me liberty or give me death" speech. We have applauded him for his eloquence, courage and foresight. Why is Colin Kaepernick not afforded the same type of respect for his courageous stand against a present-day abuse of power? Why is Kaepernick not likewise embraced for standing up to what he perceives to be heartless indifference? Why is there a seemingly contrasting response to Kaepernick's opposition to perceived abuse versus the response we have for Samuel Adams and The

Sons of Liberty along with the fiery rhetoric of Patrick Henry?

We talk about freedom, and the implication is that we are all free because we as African people no longer suffer under the weight of physical bondage. But the reality is that there are numerous forms of enslavement. So if, for instance, I tell you that you can vote for any candidate in a political race that you prefer, but I hold a gun to your head each time you attempt to vote for one candidate and I leave you alone when you began to show that you are about to vote for the other, then your choice is forced: you vote a certain way or die. This is an example where true freedom is not being exercised. It is not being exercised because there are terrible consequences if you don't cast your vote for a certain candidate. True freedom comes with the understanding that you not only have the right to protest or provide a dissenting view, but along with that comes the belief that you will not be subjected to harm if you disagree, nor will your loved ones or your property be damaged. The threat of damage or harm due to an opposing view is in fact the antithesis of freedom. If this type of culture exists, we must truly question if we are allowing freedom to take place. This is one of the things that bother me most about many people's response to Kaepernick. So many of my European brethren have said they will not watch the NFL if Kaepernick is still playing. One friend of mine, whose team has players that have likewise started taking a knee to protest in unison with Kaepernick, has stated that he will no longer watch his favorite football team even though he is a lifelong fan. It is fine to disagree, but boycotting because someone is standing up to historical excessive force is probably not the most caring - or level headed- stance to take.

This also concerns me because our response is consistent with the blame- the- victim mentality we have in this country. For instance, if a woman is unfortunately raped, the first things we want to ask are: "How much did she have to drink? Was she known to be a 'loose' woman? Where was she when the rape took place? Did she tease the man? Was she dressed provocatively?" It is as if we want to blame her for the man's inability to conduct himself in a humane manner, and thus remove any sense of responsibility from the crime doer. We often do the same thing with African Americans. Anytime we attempt to peacefully verbalize our discontent with something, we are often told to "go back to Africa" before we can complete the sentence. I hope and pray one day we will develop the ability to hear the pleas of the victims of abuse and not immediately grow cold and defensive. If a woman is saying she was raped, it does not mean that she is categorizing all men similarly. Likewise, when Kaepernick protests excessive force by some police, he is not saying all police are crooked. He knows full well the challenges that go along with the job, and I am sure he will clarify, as I will, that there are plenty of great police officers that perform their duties courageously and admirably. That is undeniable. That awareness, however, does not justify us excusing instances of excessive force or shows of disregard for human life when those incidents occur.

I want to conclude by saying that protest is necessary. Let us take the case of Curt Flood. Who was Curt Flood? He was an outfielder for the St. Louis Cardinals in the 1960s. At the latter part of his career, the Cardinals attempted to trade Curt to Philadelphia. He was opposed to the trade and sought the assistance of a lawyer. At the time players had no say in the matter when it came to their professional baseball careers. Whatever team initially landed a player had the rights to that player for their entire playing career, unless the team decided to cut or trade the player. Either way, players had no say as far as what would be done with their careers. Curt saw this as being opposed to the free market concept that is a component of capitalism. Being an intelligent man and understanding the basics of economics, Mr. Flood believed that a player had the right to make his services available to competing bodies and that the athlete's talent and current market value should determine the salary that they would acquire, and not the arbitrary payment that some owner felt comfortable giving to a player, which was often far beneath what the player would receive if their services were competed for. By having rules in place that ensured players had no leverage to elevate their salaries according to their value, owners would historically pay players significantly less than a fair portion of the money that players generated for the organization. Mr. Flood understood that people watch the game because of the players, not the owners. Fans purchase tickets because of the players' performance, not because of the stylishness of an owner's dress suit. Replicas of star players' jerseys were purchased because of the admiration someone had for the way the athletes played the game. Mr. Flood recognized that the players were generating a far larger share of the profits than what they were compensated for. It is for these reasons that he sought to challenge professional baseball's stranglehold on players' careers. Curt's defiant stance against baseball created the environment that led to increased awareness to the fact that baseball was essentially treating players like property with no say. Primarily because of Curt's courageous challenge of the system, free agency in professional baseball became a reality. Players' salaries skyrocketed, and attendance did as well, probably due to the excitement of knowing that your favorite team now had a chance to acquire more talented players due to their increased availability. All players who are paid handsomely today owe a debt of gratitude to Curt Flood for his visionary stand. His personal protest has ensured that all players (regardless of ethnicity) can earn what they are worth.

Lastly, let us remember that we have three branches of government (executive, legislative, and judicial). Our forefathers structured the government that way so that checks and balances are inherent in the system. This makes it less likely that one branch will assume too much power and become tyrannical with the power that they wield. Similarly, in society we have corporations, the police force, businesses and we have the general masses. There are times when the more powerful elements of our society have callously treated members of the general population. Without protest, the examples of abuse go unknown to most and end up going uncorrected. Only through some sort of protest can the mistreatment be brought to light. It is at this point that we have an awareness that a problem exists. Our next step is to see what can be done to rectify the issue. Protest is the "check" that balances out the tendencies of the more powerful elements of our society. It helps to prompt them to treat us more fairly, or their misdeeds will be made public.

Shouldn't we all embrace protest, and thus freedom of speech?

What My Wife Has Taught Me

1. **People are creatures of habit**. People seem to do things the same way over and again. I think it is a matter of comfort. We do not seem to like to try to do things differently because that often requires additional learning or a new mental orientation. We often seem opposed to that, and that opposition appears to intensify with age. However, I digress. The point is if you study peoples' habits you can often make your life simpler. For instance, if you noticed that a friend of yours is not good about being on time, make a mental note of that. In the future if you have a need to be met but it must be done in a timely fashion, do not ask the person who has a disregard for time to handle that situation. They will likely only frustrate you. Sometimes we allow our love for others to prompt us to make emotional decisions and put people in situations that are not consistent with that person's habits. If we make objective decisions with a person's habits in mind, it just may simplify our lives. Additionally, observing habits can help you avoid problems. For example, if a female notices a guy that she is attracted to has had a history of being physically abusive, she would be wise to allow that awareness to prompt her to steer clear of a relationship with the gentleman. Regardless of how kind he has been thus far, it is likely that the habit of being overly forceful in prior relationships is going to manifest itself at some point, particularly if the man in question has not received counseling for this type of behavior.

2. **Things are seldom black and white**. There is often a great deal of grey area. For example, my current employment requires that I deliver to peoples' homes. When someone moves away from a house on my delivery route, I sometimes receive a notification from the departing residents that they are moving to a new address. This alerts me to attempt to send any mailings to the forwarding address (assuming they provided one). The forwarding notification that I receive tells me that the move was a "family" move or an "individual' move. In other words, if a couple leaves a home they can notify me that the "Johnson" family has moved. If only the husband has moved, for instance, the move notification form may indicate that an individual forward for Kevin Johnson has taken place. This means that Mrs. Johnson will continue to receive items from me at the current address. It is only Kevin's mail that I will attempt to forward. If Kevin, however, incorrectly indicates on the forward notification form that the move reflects that a family departure took place even though only he has left, I will forward all the mail because that's what the forwarding notification instructs me to do. I am not aware that Mrs. Johnson is still there. When she subsequently receives no mail, she may call on the phone, angry, telling my supervisor about my lack of attentiveness and general incompetence. Had she taken a deep breath, slowed down and considered the grey area (the details), she would have been alerted to the fact that Kevin filled out the forward

notification incorrectly and I was simply following the instructions I had received. If we stop thinking in terms of black and white and consider all the possibilities before we become hostile, we may find that there is more involved than we had considered.

3. **You get what you pay for**. This is so simplistic but so true. We may go to a Family Dollar store and purchase an inexpensive item like a stapler or a hole puncher with the thinking that we can save a buck by purchasing an inexpensive version of the item. However, it is not unusual for cheap items to break down shortly after purchase. Yes, it appeared that the less expensive stapler or hole puncher would do just as well as something you could have purchased from Office Max, but you were sadly mistaken. I have concluded that there is a reason that some products are less expensive than similar products, even though on the surface there appears to be no significant difference. I think what we find is that the cheaper item is often made of a lower quality material, one that is less sturdy and not as reliable. Additionally, the more expensive product may have required a higher level of skill to manufacture. Furthermore, the material for the more expensive item may require more effort to obtain which may also drive up the price. All these factors probably drive up the expenses associated with the product. The business then simply passes along the costs to us by way of higher prices to

cover their expenses. So, we must recognize that sometimes it may be better to pay a little more (within reason) just to minimize the headache of having something break down on us shortly after purchase and being burdened with the fact that we must go right back out and purchase a more reliable version of what just broke.

Four Things I Would Tell Young People

(A co-worker not long ago pulled me aside. We talk about various things pertaining to life and self-advancement on occasion. On this day, he asked what things I would pass along to our youth if I were asked to do so. I asked him to let me sleep on it and that I would try to bring him a response the following day. I went home, turned off the television and the radio and isolated myself from distractions for a short while. Here is a list of the things I gave my friend the following day.)

1. **Spirituality is a must**. It does not matter what system you adopt, although I suggest you consider indigenous systems of worship. The key is to strive to develop the depth of spiritual awareness that allows you to see how small our daily troubles are in comparison to the vastness and limitlessness of the universe.

2. **Obtain some sort of practical, hands on skills** (locksmithing, plumbing, automobile repair, computer networking or repair, auto body repair, HVAC, electrician, etc.), so that if this society does not hire you, you will be able to start your own business and work for yourself.

3. **Follow your passion**. Indulge in your passion and despite all the turmoil that this life can bring for people, following your passion will give you a spark of joy, something to look forward to, that can help carry you through your day. Your circumstances may dictate that you don't have a lot of time to donate to your passion. That's understood. Just do what you love when you can, and if

you can figure out a way to generate income or make a living from your passion, that's all the better.

4. **Serve**. I believe that when you give to an activity that benefits others, it brings you peace in knowing that you have contributed somehow to humanity.

The Truth

(The following three raps were written by me with the sole purpose of keeping my writing skills as a rapper sharp while also providing me an outlet to express my feelings at all three respective moments. I hope you enjoy. By the way, much love to Kevin Sabio for providing the inspiration to include my raps. Brother Sabio had included entire songs in his book, complete with verses and hooks. My words are not from completed songs, just random recorded thoughts in rhyme. I had not initially written any of the three subsequent raps with the intention of including them in this series of essays. However, upon reading these forms of urban poetry, I concluded that they may be too good to stay confined to a notebook full of random raps. I concluded that maybe the public would be interested in some of my thoughts in moments of quiet. Only then had I realized that Brother Sabio had already done something similar before me. To him I give a mad shout out for the blueprint.)

Eliminate obstacles. Maximize potential/ I speak the truth daily. Some find it offensive/Never my intention. I choose to enlighten/We're used to the darkness. Bright lights tend to frighten/ I recognize the tendency/ But spit the truth frequently/Black and I'm proud. I'm the new Public Enemy/No menace to society/ Just spit the rhyme endlessly/ You opposed to progress, can never be a friend of me/ Compare apples to oranges. They're two different fruits/ You can't say I'm angry just because I speak truths/ Just social commentary. I verbalize what's real/ How some are traumatized, subjected to ordeals/ Your anger is misdirected. You label me the culprit/ I never harmed anyone through political bullshit/ Never raped a female or took another's land/ Never made one ashamed that he is African/ Never took someone's language, God, or religion/ I just acknowledge history. Now I need exorcisms? / I'm spiritual as they come. All tasks are directed/by the will of God. I'm just a man perfecting/ Growing in divinity/ Embracing my destiny/ If this makes me racist, then I'll embrace this willingly/

Introspection

At times I grow sad. Life's not always been kind/ Still I shine and recognize it's a friend of mine/ The concept of opposites: The joy. The pain/ The sun. The rain/ The glory. The shame/To accomplish. To fail/ To keep quiet. To tell/ To hold my breath. Exhale/ To sink. To sail/ To grow. Stay stagnant/ To repulse. Be magnets/ Dull expressions. Magnetic/ Quite lethargic. Athletic/ (pause). Sometimes I wonder why I was made into flesh/ Misunderstood but God knows that I always do my best/ Then again the universe has its own teaching means/ Sometimes for you to have peace you have to make it through the screams/ Perfect lives with no struggle provide no impetus to learn/ To look within daily and to grow more concerned/ To study life's mysteries, the questions of reality/ I now know it's struggle that's really going to challenge me/ Makes me dig deeper. Analyze life's dynamics/Why some seem to prosper, while others barely manage/ In developing this awareness maybe I gain god consciousness/ Drop a little science in a song make a monster hit/ Until I transition, guess I'll continue silent travel/ The road to understanding, whether smooth, rough or gravel/ I just need a friend. Can I confide in you/ Will you take it to the grave? Are you true through and through/ Will you turn Judas and betray me for some trinkets or a benefit/ Love is what we make it and the love could be so limitless/ But darkness is so prevalent. We must balance out the beast/ The devil's always working so our fight should never cease/

Whirlwind

A million things to do, and not enough time to do 'em/ Sometimes I feel like a major storm is straight brewin'/Winds of disturbance as they swirl in my brain/The collection of thoughts often drives me insane/Feels like a whirlwind deep inside my head/Peace eludes me until I sleep in my bed/ States of consciousness rarely finds me at ease/ Consciousness brings the whirlwind that won't cease/ I could do nothing and be non-committal/ Provide nothing to mankind, but then I would belittle/Myself in the process, not maximizing talents. Not pursuing my destiny/ Is that the place I need to be/ I think not. It's a choice of destiny or conceding/ Falling short to my purpose when destiny I believe in/ It's the burden I bare, a product of awareness/Consciousness prevents the soldier from getting careless/ And so many I talk to, or try to engage/Have no clue of the struggle. It used to leave me amazed/ Now I've learned as I've grown what you know controls responses/ Some want to be divine, but their thoughts make them monsters/ Can't ever have discussions on matters that exceed/ People's current wisdom, so more soldiers do I need/ I Keep a "to do" list so as to keep me more focused/But the list grows ever longer/ At times I grow hopeless/I can't move quick enough to dwindle all of the duties/ Time to call on my God. Here he comes to salute me/

Additional Thoughts

"Never underestimate the power of saying a kind or complimentary word to someone. That word may be the motivation that individual needs to fuel them to do things they may never have done prior to the compliment. This newly inspired individual may now in turn send a kind word to someone else, knowing from experience how the compliment they received elevated them. If we can continue this habit, can you imagine the power that this simple gesture can have on people, and ultimately humanity?"

"Why is it that you can attend church every Sunday, and the pastor is telling you essentially the same thing (Pray to God and everything will fall into place for you.)? You do not question this strategy, believing mere prayer will change your conditions in this physical realm. However, when someone other than your Pastor provides practical, real life strategies to elevate your conditions, you call them 'preachy.'

I had recently purchased a copy of People magazine (May 2016) commemorating the life of the great musical artist, Prince Roger Nelson. The cashier jokingly said "this is an ugly cover" and further inquired if I was sure I wanted to pay over $15 for the magazine. She said, "Prince never gave me any money. Did he give you any money?" I said with a smile, "No, but he touched my soul. How much is that worth?"

"A woman's sexiest aspects are not her hips, buttocks or the fullness of her bosom. Those things only catch your eye. Her real sex appeal, those aspects that transcend time, is found in the goodness of her heart, the strength of her mind, and the depth of her spiritual awareness."

"One basic interpretation of Karma is that the energy you send out is what you will receive. That being the case, why are some of us so reluctant to give love unconditionally and then complain when we don't receive the very thing we neglect to radiate?"

"If you get challenged by a greyhound, you do not indulge him in a footrace. You cannot win. You become victorious by changing the nature of the competition to one that utilizes the maximization of your particular skills. Never play to your enemy's strength."

"Being the outsider is not necessarily a bad thing. Being outside affords you the opportunity to view things from a different perspective. In the process, it increases the likelihood that you will be able to see things that others do not."

"Being dismissive of what you do not understand could be interpreted by some as arrogance."

"Too often we respond from an emotional or speculative place when putting forth answers to social problems. A better strategy is to objectively go about the process of identifying the root cause of the problem. Only then are we armed with the information needed to form a corrective plan."

"There appears to be three universal languages: mathematics, music and telepathy. The mastering of one or all three should enhance one's capacity to communicate with other higher intelligences, even those from other galaxies or realms."

"Take two things of equal value, and make one of those things appear to be inaccessible. Take the other thing that is equally valuable and make it readily available. Chances are that people will expend a great deal of energy trying to obtain the more elusive of the two."

"We are quick to talk about gun control as a means to curb violence, but are a lot less enthusiastic to discuss two things: 1. the socio-economic conditions that increase the likelihood that crime will take place, 2. the feelings of isolation, despair, bullying and abuse that often precede acts of violence."

"The tragedy is not necessarily the fact that unfortunate events occur. The real tragedy may be to go through that unpleasant experience and come out of it no more informed than you were going in."

"If someone has told you before that you are talented or gifted in some way, and this same individual tends to try to nudge you to have the courage to do certain things, understand that they may not be trying to give you a hard time. Maybe they simply see greatness in you and want to help you access that greatness and bring it to the surface."

"If we are made in God's image, but you hate the reflection of yourself in the mirror, what does that suggest?'

"The hardest thing to do in life is not to beat anyone down or to show how physically imposing you are. The hardest thing to do is to survive the many sources of pain and challenges that this life can throw at you and somehow still maintain a sense of compassion, decency and unselfishness."

"No one is perfect. However, I do think that we are influenced both directly and indirectly by the energies of those with whom we associate. That being the case, isn't it a good idea to form a circle of associates whose primary mental approach to life is one of positivity and service?"

"One of the most difficult things about being an African is that every crime that we commit or every behavior that is less than ideal is seen as confirmation of our inherently lower evolutionary status. However, any time we do something that is exceptional, particularly if the accomplishment is of an intellectual nature; it is seen as an aberration instead of proof of our ability to do all things when obstacles are eliminated from our paths."

Quotes

"I am no better than any man, but I AM as good as everyman."

"A lie told often enough, especially if it is promoted through the media, at some point begins to assume the appearance of truth."

"When lies continue to go uncorrected, our existence at some point becomes no more than a colossal fabrication."

"Before you can shine, you must first polish up your act."

"Our biggest obstacle to forward progress is not always racism. Sometimes our biggest impediment is our own lack of belief in self."

"Power, authority and advanced spiritual knowledge should only be given to those individuals that have demonstrated the needed self-love, humility, selflessness, and commitment to humanity to use that understanding and power for the improvement of others and not the exploitation of them."

"Physical liberation in the absence of economic liberation only gives the illusion of freedom."

"You can take away a man's home, source of income, spouse and even his life, but you cannot take away his integrity. That must be conceded."

"Judge a man not by one bad deed or statement, but by the totality of his works."

"Just because a man does not have in his possession a gun or a hand grenade does not mean that he is not engaged in combat."

"Do only what's needed to survive and feel like a slave marching to an inevitable grave. Follow your dreams and passions, and feel much like the eagle soaring on the currents, looking down on the earth while admiring the beauty."

"You can improve the quality of your life significantly by elevating the nature of your thoughts and being selective of your associates."

"The mouth is a powerful tool. Used correctly, it can be the source of conflict resolution. Used incorrectly, it can be the source of a terrible mishap."

"Forgive others. Forgive yourself, and love unconditionally despite past betrayals."

"There are no obstacles. There are only OPPORTUNITIES for growth, elevation and expansion."

"At one point I almost lost everything, but in the process I found myself."

"The deeper we dig, the greater the odds that we will uncover a buried treasure."

"Ignoring an ugly truth does not make that unpleasant reality any less real."

"The only thing worse than ignorance is the arrogance that usually comes with it."

"Stroking your own ego is nothing but mental masturbation."

"Discomfort is a prerequisite to growth."

"If you do not know the difference between arrogance and confidence, you're probably a little on the arrogant side."

"If you keep sweeping things under the rug, the accumulation of filth will ultimately cause you to fall."

References

Afrika, L. (1983). *African Holistic Health*. Brooklyn: A & B Publishers Group.

Amen, R. (1990). *Metu Neter*. Brooklyn: Khamit Corporation.

Bennett, L. (1961). *Before the Mayflower*: Johnson Publishing Company.

Imhotep, D. Ph.D. (2011). *The First Americans Were Africans*. Bloomington: AuthorHouse.

Kinnebrew, K. (2015, February 13). Albert Einstein Endorses Black History Month? *BlackNews.Com*. Retrieved March 10, 2016, from http://www.blacknews.com/news/albert-einstein-endorses-black-history-month/#.WHJdwYWcGUk.

Kwesi, A. & Kwesi, M. (1995). *Afrikan Builders of Civilization*. Dallas: Kemet Nu Productions.

Pimenta-Bey (2002). *Othello's Children in the "New World."* 1st Books.

Price, S. (2015, December21). Sportsperson of the Year. *Sports Illustrated, 123*, 66-87.

Links to Afi Makalani on Social Media

Music:

https://www.reverbnation.com/afimakalani

http://afimakalani.com/

Twitter:

@AfiMakalani

LinkedIn:

Afi Makalani

Instagram:

https://www.instagram.com/afimakalani/